THE CHEF OF KINGS, THE KING OF CHEFS

A Novel Inspired by the Life and Legacy of Antoine-Marie Carême

"Sugar, Power, and the First Celebrity Chef Who Conquered Europe: A Legacy Forged in Flour and Fire"

Dorian Cainewell

Published by DC Publishing
ISBN: 978-1-0692330-0-4 (Hardcover)

Cover design and Editing by Hmd Publishing
First Edition Printed in Canada 2025

Dedication

To my family, whose legacies have inspired me to dream, create, and strive for greatness.

To my great-great-grandfather, who carried the first Torah to Calgary, and to my great-grandfather, whose ingenuity birthed the iconic Smithbilt hat and the symbol of Calgary, the white cowboy hat. Your pioneering spirits are woven into the very fabric of this story, reminding me that courage and vision can shape the identity of a city and beyond.

To my grandfather, Irwin A. Blackstone, a champion of justice and intellect, whose work as a provincial court judge and namesake of the Blackstone Debates at the University of Calgary exemplifies a life devoted to integrity and influence.

To my family, who nurtured a deep love of music, Artists, and heritage, enriching the cultural landscape of Calgary and leaving an indelible mark on every stage, every classroom, and everyone they touched.

To the countless chefs, dreamers, and creators who dare to see art in the everyday and infuse their work with purpose and passion.

And finally, to you, the reader, for taking this journey into the life of a man who shaped history with sugar and flour and whose legacy reminds us all that creativity and perseverance can endure beyond time.

This book is a tribute to ambition, artistry, and the enduring power of legacy. Thank you for believing in the story I have poured my heart into.

"The fine arts are five in number: painting, sculpture, poetry, music, and architecture, whose principal branch is confectionery."
—Antoine Marie Carême, L'Art de la Cuisine Française au Dix-Neuvième Siècle

Acknowledgments

Creating *The Chef of Kings* has been an extraordinary journey, and it would not have been possible without the support, inspiration, and contributions of many individuals and institutions. I am deeply grateful for the guidance, encouragement, and resources that made this novel a reality.

First and foremost, I wish to express my gratitude to the culinary historians, archivists, and writers who have preserved the legacy of Antoine Carême and his era. The works of scholars such as Ian Kelly and Marie-Antoine Lefèvre provided invaluable insights into Carême's life, philosophies, and the cultural context of 19th-century France. Their dedication to uncovering and sharing this history allowed me to bring Carême's genius vividly to life.

A heartfelt thanks also go to modern chefs, pâtissiers, and culinary educators who continue celebrating Carême's legacy. Their passion for innovation, coupled with their respect for tradition, inspired many aspects of this story. Their work is a testament to the enduring relevance of Carême's contributions to haute cuisine.

This novel would not have been possible without the unwavering support of my family, friends, and mentors. To my loved ones, thank you for believing in me and this story, for listening to my ideas, and for encouraging me to keep going even when the road seemed daunting. Your faith in my work gave me the strength to see this project through.

To my early readers and beta readers, your thoughtful feedback was invaluable. You challenged me to dig deeper, to enrich the characters, and to make *The Chef of Kings* as immersive and compelling as possible. Your insights and enthusiasm shaped this book in ways I cannot fully express.

I also owe a tremendous debt to <u>HmdPublishing</u> and team. Your meticulous attention to detail, insightful suggestions, and unwavering dedication to bringing this story to life have been nothing short of extraordinary. Thank you for believing in this vision and helping to refine it into its final form.

This novel is as much a reflection of my personal history as it is a tribute to Antoine Carême. To my family, whose roots in Calgary, Alberta, span over a century, thank you for inspiring me with your stories of resilience, creativity, and dedication. From my great-great-grandfather, who brought Calgary's first Torah, to my great-grandfather, who founded Smithbilt Hats and created the iconic white cowboy hat, your legacies have reminded me of the importance of dreaming boldly and contributing meaningfully.

To my grandfather, Irwin A. Blackstone, whose legacy in law and education continues to inspire through the annual Blackstone Debates, thank you for showing me the value of intellectual curiosity and integrity. I hope this work honors the spirit of your contributions in its own way.

Finally, to you, the reader: thank you for taking the time to explore this story and Antoine Carême's remarkable journey. Your imagination and curiosity breathe life into these pages. It is my hope that this novel not only entertains but also inspires you to reflect on your own dreams, passions, and legacies.

Antoine's dream began not in opulence but in the cramped bakery where every loaf of bread held a lesson in perseverance. Carême believed that creation was a way to connect with the eternal, to leave a piece of oneself behind for others to discover. I hope this story serves as a bridge—a connection between the past, present, and future. This novel is a tribute to those who have courage and those who dare to build their castles, whether in kitchens or in life.

CONTENTS

PART 1.
THE APPRENTICE'S BEGINNINGS AND ASCENT

PART 2.
THE CHEF OF KINGS

PART 3.
THE PHILOSOPHER OF FOOD

PART 4. A LEGACY DEFINED

PART 5.
THE EXPANDING FLAME

PART 6.
THE GLOBAL TABLE

FOREWORD

As a chef, I have spent years immersed in the artistry and discipline of kitchens. My journey in professional kitchens has taught me not just the mechanics of cooking but the profound connection between creativity, culture, and the indomitable spirit. It is this connection that inspired me to write *The Chef of Kings*.

Antoine Carême, often regarded as the first celebrity chef, has always been a figure of fascination for me. His ability to elevate cooking to an art form, his visionary approach to presentation, and his relentless ambition resonate deeply with anyone who has ever set foot in a professional kitchen. Through his life and work, Carême not only shaped the future of cuisine but also showed us the limitless possibilities of creativity.

In this novel, I have sought to blend historical fact with fiction to explore not only the events of Carême's life but also the emotions, struggles, and triumphs that may have defined him as a person. My hope is that this story serves as a tribute to the man, the chef, the creator, and to all those who continue to innovate and inspire.

To my fellow chefs and dreamers: May this novel remind you that every creation carries a piece of your soul; through that, your story can live on forever.

Dorian Cainewell

AUTHOR'S NOTES

Writing *The Chef of Kings* has been both an enriching journey and a labor of love. Antoine Carême's life and achievements serve as a testament to the power of dedication, spirit, and resilience, and it has been a privilege to weave a narrative that celebrates his extraordinary legacy. This novel is the culmination of extensive historical research, creative interpretation, and a deep appreciation for the culture in which Carême lived.

Historical Sources and Research Methods

To bring Antoine Carême's realm to life, I immersed myself in a wealth of primary and secondary historical resources. Among the materials I consulted were:

- **Antoine Carême own writings**, *L'Art de la Cuisine Française au Dix-Neuvième Siècle* and *Le Pâtissier Royal Parisien* were invaluable for understanding his culinary philosophies, techniques, and the aesthetic principles that shaped his work.

- **Culinary histories and biographies**: Books such as *The Kings of Pastry* by Marie-Antoine Lefèvre and *Cooking for Kings: The Life of Antonin Carême* by Ian Kelly provided context on Carême's role in the evolution of haute cuisine and his interactions with notable historical figures.

- **Archival material**: Research into 19th-century European courts, particularly those of France, Russia, and England, was essential in recreating the settings and power dynamics that defined Carême's professional life.

- **Period-specific culinary techniques**: Studies of early 19th-century French cooking practices, including sugar work and pâtisserie, helped ground the novel's depictions of Carême's craft in historical accuracy.

- **Historical records of Paris**: Maps, architectural drawings, and written accounts of Paris in the early 1800s were referenced to authentically portray the city that served as the backdrop to Carême's rise.

Bridging History and Creativity

While rooted in thorough research, *The Chef of Kings* is a work of historical fiction. Certain characters, dialogues, and events have been fictionalized or embellished to enhance the narrative and explore Carême's inner world. These creative liberties were taken with great care to ensure that they complemented the historical framework rather than detracting from it.

In constructing the story's interpersonal relationships and emotional arcs, I sought to humanize Carême, imagining the joys, struggles, and ambitions that might have shaped the man behind the legend. I also sought to highlight the cultural and societal forces at play during his time, underscoring the role of cuisine as both an art form and a reflection of political and social currents.

Closing Reflections

Antoine Carême's story is not just about food—it is about transformation and the enduring power of creation. In writing this novel, I hoped to capture the universal truths embodied in his life: the pursuit of beauty, the importance of legacy, and the courage to dream.

I invite readers to immerse themselves, not only to marvel at his culinary brilliance but also to reflect on how art—whether through food, words, or any other medium—has the power to transcend time and connect us across generations.

Dorian Cainewell

PROLOGUE: THE FIRE WITHIN

The narrow streets of Paris were cloaked in darkness, the only light coming from the flickering glow of lanterns and the faint gleam of moonlight reflecting off cobblestones. The scent of freshly baked bread wafted through the cool night air, mingling with the distant murmur of the Seine. The city, though quiet, was alive in its own way, its heartbeat steady even as everything and everyone slumbered.

Inside a small bakery tucked between stone buildings, a boy sat at a wooden table, his fingers smudged with flour and ink. By the dim light of a single candle, he sketched furiously, his hand moving across the paper as if guided by something greater than himself. The drawing took shape: towering arches of spun sugar, delicate columns of caramel, and intricate details that seemed impossible to create yet felt destined to exist.

This boy was Antoine Carême, an orphan who had found refuge in the warmth of ovens and the rhythm of dough. To others, he was merely an apprentice, a helper who swept floors and fetched water. But to himself, he was something more. He was a dreamer, an artist, and, above all, a believer in the transformative power of beauty.

The bakery door creaked open, and the chill of the night spilled in as the baker, Monsieur Bailly, entered.

He paused when he saw Antoine hunched over his sketches, his brow furrowed in concentration. "Still awake, boy?" Bailly's voice was gruff but not unkind. Antoine looked up, startled, and quickly tried to hide his drawings. But Bailly waved a hand, stepping closer to the table. "Let me see," the baker said, his tone softer now.

Reluctantly, Antoine slid the paper toward him. Bailly studied the sketches for a long moment, his expression unreadable. Then, with a small nod, he set the paper back down.

"You've got an eye for detail," Bailly said. "And ambition, too. But too much can burn as hot as an oven. Keep it stoked, boy, but don't let it consume you." Antoine's cheeks flushed, but he met the baker's gaze with unwavering determination. "I want to create something that lasts, Monsieur. Something that people will remember long after the taste has faded." Bailly's lips twitched into a faint smile. "Then you'll need more than skill. You'll need discipline, patience, and the courage to stand tall when society tries to tear you down." The weight of the baker's words settled over him.

Voiceover (Older Antoine): *"That night, in the dim glow of Bailly's bakery, I made a silent vow. I would carve my name into history—not with ink, but with sugar and fire."*

As the candles flicker lower, Antoine returned to his sketches, his hand steady despite the late hour. Each line he drew felt like a step toward a future he could almost grasp. Somewhere beyond the darkness of those Parisian streets lay grandeur, and Antoine Carême was determined to claim his place within it.

Antoine Carême's vision took shape long before he touched his first piece of sugar. As he looked at the crude sketches in his hands, he whispered to himself, "One day, they will stand as tall as kings.

PART I
THE APPRENTICE'S BEGINNINGS AND ASCENT

CHAPTER 1
THE BOY AND THE BAKERY

Paris, 1794. The streets of Paris smelled of fresh bread, horse manure, and desperation. Antoine's stomach growled as he shuffled past bakeries, each window teasing him with glimpses of loaves he couldn't afford. He pressed the sketches closer to his chest, a shield against both hunger and doubt.

The city groaned under the weight of its own revolution. Smoke curled from the crumbled facades of once-grand buildings, mingling with hawkers' shouts and the destitute groans. Barefoot children darted through the crowded streets, their faces smudged with soot and hunger, clutching scraps of stolen bread. Among them was Antoine Carême, ten years old and utterly alone. Antoine's frame was small for his age, his ribs visible beneath the threadbare shirt he wore. His lively, sharp eyes were his only defense against the chaos of the city. In his pocket, folded carefully to avoid damage, was his greatest treasure: a sketch of an opulent palace he had drawn on a scrap of parchment scavenged from the gutter. He often traced the lines of the turrets and arches with a dirty fingertip, imagining a life beyond the misery that enveloped him. The streets of Paris were not kind to dreamers. But Antoine's hands, calloused and unwavering, were already sketching the foundations of his future. Today, however, he had little time for dreaming. Hunger gnawed at his stomach, sharper than the winter wind that sliced through the constricting alleys.

Antoine crouched behind a rickety fruit stall, fixed on a bruised apple near the edge of the vendor's table. He licked his cracked lips, counting to three in his head, before darting forward. The apple was within his grasp when a gnarled hand closed around his wrist.

"Thief!" the vendor roared, his voice rough with years of barking prices over the marketplace din. Antoine squirmed, trying to free himself, but the man's grip was iron. "Please, monsieur," Antoine gasped, his voice high and desperate. "I'll starve if I don't eat." "Then starve like the rest of them," the vendor growled. He yanked the apple from Antoine's hand and raised his other arm, ready to strike. Before the blow could land, a shadow fell across them both. "What's all this noise about?" a deep, gruff voice demanded. The vendor froze, his gaze widening as he looked up at the man who had intervened.

Sylvain Bailly, a stout baker with flour streaked across his apron and arms as thick as tree trunks, stood with his hands on his hips. His expression was stern, but his stare lingered on Antoine with something resembling curiosity. "This little rat was trying to steal from me," the vendor said, his voice losing some of its fire. Bailly grunted. "He doesn't look like much of a thief to me. Just a hungry boy. Let him go." The vendor released Antoine reluctantly, muttering under his breath. Antoine stumbled backward, clutching his wrist and eyeing Bailly warily.

"What's your name, boy?" Bailly asked, his tone brusque but not unkind. "Antoine, monsieur," he whispered, his voice barely audible over the din of the market. Bailly glanced over to the crumpled sketch poking out of Antoine's pocket. "What's that?" Antoine hesitated, then pulled it out, smoothing the folds with care. "A palace," he said simply, holding it up for Bailly to see. The baker's bushy eyebrows lifted. "You drew this?" Antoine's heart was pounding in his chest. He had never shown the drawing to anyone before.

Bailly studied it for a moment before grunting again. "You've got fire in you, boy. Come to my bakery tomorrow. If you can keep from burning the place down, I might find some work for you." Antoine stared at him, unsure whether to trust the offer. But the growl of his stomach made the decision for him. "Thank you, monsieur," he said, his voice trembling with a mixture of relief and disbelief. Bailly waved a hand dismissively. "Don't thank me yet. Show up on time, or the offer's off the table." As Bailly walked away, Antoine clutched his sketch and watched the baker's broad back disappear into the crowd. For the first time in years, a flicker of hope stirred within him. He had been given a chance—one he would not squander.

The next morning, Antoine arrived at Bailly's bakery just as the sun rose. The warm glow of the ovens lit the windows, and the scent of fresh bread filled the street. Antoine hesitated at the door before stepping inside. The bakery pulsed with energy, the heat of the ovens radiating through the stone walls. The air carried the scent of yeast and caramelized sugar, mingling with the steady thud of kneading dough and the sharp clang of metal trays. Apprentices darted between stations; their movements were practiced and precise.

Bailly barely looked up as Antoine stepped inside. "You're early," he muttered, tossing a clean apron in his direction. "Good. That means you're serious. Let's see if you can keep up."

Antoine caught the apron, tying it firmly around his waist. His first task was simple: cracking eggs into a bowl. He focused, but his fingers trembled, his grip uncertain. The first egg shattered in his hands, dripping yolk onto the counter. Bailly's voice cut through the din. "Gentle, boy. You're not breaking stones." Antoine swallowed hard, nodding. He wiped his hands, grabbed another egg, and this time, he cracked it cleanly. One small victory. "Careful, boy," Bailly growled, looming over him. "We don't waste food here." Antoine swallowed hard with a slight gesture of affirmation, determined not to make another mistake.

As the hours passed, he found his rhythm. He learned to move quickly but deliberately, his small hands becoming steady and precise. By the end of the day, his arms ached, and his clothes were dusted with flour, but he felt a flicker of pride. That night, after the bakery had closed and the apprentices had gone home, Antoine sat alone by the dying embers of the oven. He pulled out his sketch and traced the lines of the palace once more, his fingers smudged with flour. Bailly, who had stayed to clean up, paused by the door and watched the boy. "You've got desire, Antoine," he said gruffly. "Desire's good. But it's no substitute for hard work. Remember that." "Yes, monsieur," Antoine replied, his voice quiet but resolute. He didn't know what the future held, but he believed he might have one. "One day," he whispered to himself, "I'll build something they'll all remember."

Outside the bakery, the stars seemed to glimmer in agreement, casting their light over the thinning streets of Paris— A city in turmoil yet showing glimpses of slow recovery, brimming with endless possibilities for a boy chasing his dream.

CHAPTER 1A
THE FIRST WEEKS

Paris, vibrant and unpredictable, was in flux. Its streets bustled with merchants peddling their wares, their cries blending with the clatter of hooves on cobblestones and the murmur of revolution still fresh in the air. It was a city where dreams were forged and broken in equal measure, a crucible that could refine or destroy. For Antoine Carême, this was a beginning. The boy who had once wandered the streets, surviving on scraps and the kindness of strangers, now stood at the threshold of something greater. Bailly's bakery was no mere shop; it was a gateway, A place Antoine could scarcely comprehend but was determined to conquer. That night before he fell asleep, the warmth of the bakery's ovens still lingering in his memory, he traced the lines of his treasured palace drawing once again. "The boy who has only survived," he whispered, "will now begin building."

His first day had been humbling. With flour coating every surface and voices overlapping in a chaotic symphony. Eager to impress, Antoine had fumbled through the simplest of tasks, his clumsiness drawing harsh reprimands from both Bailly and the older apprentices. Yet, even as humiliation singed his cheeks, something within him refused to yield.

Voiceover (Older Antoine): *"When I first stepped into Bailly's bakery, I knew nothing. I didn't know how to hold a rolling pin properly, let alone bake something worth selling. I was just another pair of hands— expendable, replaceable. But deep down, I knew I wasn't. I would make* *myself indispensable. Failure wasn't an option; it was simply another lesson to master."*

Antoine's first weeks were a trial of endurance. He woke before dawn, every muscle aching, and stumbled into the bakery's warmth. The morning air still held a bite, but inside, the ovens blazed, and the day's work had already begun.

His tasks were endless—sweeping flour-dusted floors, scrubbing mixing bowls until his fingers pruned, carrying sacks of flour heavier than himself. The other apprentices moved like clockwork, barely sparing him a glance. Antoine kept his head down, absorbing everything—the way Bailly tested dough with a single touch, the rhythm of folding butter into the pastry, the scent of sugar caramelizing at just the right temperature.

At night, while the others collapsed into sleep, Antoine sat near the dying embers of the oven, sketching by candlelight. His first drawings were crude, the lines uneven. But as the weeks passed, his strokes grew bolder, his visions sharper. He wasn't just imagining desserts—he was designing them.

Often, he'd trace the lines of his palace drawing, now smudged with flour and slightly torn, and weave its grandeur into his pastry designs. The same soaring turrets and intricate arches began to appear in his sketches of sugar towers and pastry structures.

Long after the bakery had emptied, Antoine remained, tracing the grooves of a rolling pin with calloused fingers. The silence was comforting, broken only by the distant crackle of cooling embers. He floured the workbench and shaped the dough, mimicking Bailly's movements as precisely as he could recall. His hands trembled slightly—he was exhausted, but he wasn't finished.

A shadow moved behind him. "What are you doing?" Bailly's gruff voice cut through the quiet. Antoine snapped upright, flour dusting his arms. "Practicing, monsieur." Bailly leaned against the counter, arms crossed. "Practicing, eh? And what exactly have you learned?" Antoine hesitated, then gestured to the dough. "I learned to handle it gently, like you said. To feel its texture, to know when it's ready—not just by time, but by touch." Bailly raised an eyebrow, stepping closer to inspect the boy's work. He pressed a finger into the dough, "Not bad. But it's far from perfect. Start again." Antoine didn't flinch. He scraped the dough off the counter, cleaned the surface, and began anew. Bailly watched silently, the corners of his mouth twitching as if suppressing a smile. For all his gruffness, the baker recognized something rare in the boy—a spark that could, if nurtured, ignite into brilliance.

Voiceover (Older Antoine): *"Bailly wasn't kind, but he was fair. He commanded perfection, and in doing so, he taught me to demand it of myself. It was there, in the quiet hours after the bakery emptied, that I began to understand what it meant to strive for greatness. It wasn't about the applause or the accolades; it was about mastering what I loved to do."*

As the weeks turned to months, Antoine's confidence grew. The tasks that had once seemed impossible became second nature. He learned to shape dough with precision, to gauge the temperature of the ovens by instinct, and to whip cream into perfect peaks. By day, he worked tirelessly to meet Bailly's exacting standards. By night, he dreamed of towering confections and grand banquets, where his creations would not merely be consumed but celebrated. His sketches became more elaborate, his ideas more daring. And though the path ahead was uncertain, Antoine knew one thing for certain: he would not be confined by the limits of what was expected. He would define his own.

Each night, as he finished his work, Antoine's thoughts returned to the crumpled palace drawing tucked beneath his cot. The soaring turrets reminded him of what was possible—of what he was working toward. With every loaf of bread and every swirl of frosting, Antoine Carême took another step closer to how the Chefs worldwide know him today.

CHAPTER 2
THE ART OF AMBITION

The bakery buzzed with its own rhythm, a symphony of clattering porcelain, the steady vibrations of the oven, and the occasional barked order from Sylvain Bailly. Antoine Carême, now a permanent fixture of this bustling circle, found himself drawn deeper into its intricacies each day. Though his hands ached and his back burned from long hours spent hunched over workbenches, his spirit soared. He was learning, and with every mistake corrected, every technique mastered, the dream that flickered within him grew brighter.

As the months continued on, he no longer hesitated with a rolling pin, nor did his hands shake when folding butter into delicate pastry layers. The movements had become second nature, and Bailly's corrections grew fewer. Yet, ambition still whispered in Antoine's ear. Late at night, when the bakery was silent, he pushed himself further, crafting elaborate designs from leftover dough and sugar scraps. Each creation was a vision of what could be, not just pastries but edible sculptures.

One night, Bailly found him hunched over a caramel lattice, the golden strands forming a delicate web. The older man said nothing at first, only watching. Then he grumbled, crossing his arms. "You have incredible energy. But that needs control. Get some rest. You'll shape nothing but ashes if you burn yourself out." Antoine wiped the sweat from his brow, nodding. But as he lay in his cot that night, staring at his sketches by candlelight, he knew he was chasing something greater than exhaustion.

Voiceover (Older Antoine): *"Those early days at Bailly's bakery were nothing short of transformative. It was there, in the heat of the ovens and the rhythm of kneading dough, that I learned the foundation of everything I would become. Bailly was not just a baker; he was a craftsman, a master of his art. His standards were impossibly high, and his speech often piercing, but he pushed me to see beyond flour and sugar—to envision beauty and precision in every creation."*

Three months into his apprenticeship, Antoine had earned a reputation among the other apprentices. They called him "Le Petit Architecte" for the detailed sketches he left scattered on scraps of parchment around the bakery. Towers of sugar, intricate arches carved from dough, and pastry domes adorned with tiny, edible carvings, all born from his vivid imagination. Though some mocked his drive, Antoine's persistence was unwavering. "Antoine! Stop daydreaming and focus!" Bailly's voice boomed from across the bakery, snapping Antoine from his reverie. He blinked down at the dough he had been absentmindedly kneading, realizing he'd let it overproof. "Sorry, Monsieur Bailly," Antoine muttered, his cheeks flushing. He quickly adjusted the dough, determined to salvage it. Bailly loomed over him a moment later, his thick arms crossed. "You have talent, boy, but talent means nothing without discipline. Do you want to build your sugar palaces? Fine. But first, learn to make bread that won't embarrass my name." "Oui, monsieur. I'll do better." Bailly grunted, his expression softening. "Good. Now clean that mess and start again. And remember, flour on the board, not on your face." The other apprentices snickered, but Antoine's focus remained firm. He wiped the counter clean, dusted it with flour, and began again. This time, his movements were precise, his attention absolute. The rhythm of kneading, folding, and shaping bread calmed his nerves. Bailly watched from a distance, his gruff demeanor hiding a flicker of approval.

Voiceover (Older Antoine): *"Bailly's lessons were harsh but necessary. Every scolding, every critique, was a step toward perfection. He taught that my hopes for the future meant nothing without skill—and that discipline was the bridge between the two."*

By the time the sun had dipped below the horizon, the bakery was quiet. The apprentices had gone, leaving Antoine alone with the lingering scent of baked goods and the soft crackle of cooling ovens. He pulled out his latest sketch, a design inspired by the classical architecture he had seen in an old book Bailly kept on a high shelf. The sketch depicted a towering confection: a layered masterpiece adorned with intricate carvings, spun sugar spires, and cascading ribbons of icing. To Antoine, it was more than a dessert. It was a statement—a testament to what he could achieve if given the chance.

"What are you working on now, Le Petit Architecte?" a familiar voice asked, startling him. Antoine spun around to see Bailly leaning against the doorframe, his expression unreadable. Antoine hesitated, clutching the parchment tightly. "Just an idea, monsieur. Something I'd like to create one day." Bailly stepped closer, his heavy footsteps echoing in the quiet room. He held out a hand, and after a moment's hesitation, Antoine passed him the sketch. Bailly studied it in silence. "Ambitious," he said finally, setting the paper down on the workbench. "But you won't get far without skill. These spires— they'll collapse if your sugar isn't tempered properly. And this base here? It's too tapered to support the weight above it." Antoine's face fell, but Bailly clapped a heavy hand on his shoulder. "That's not to say it's impossible. You've got the vision, boy. Now, you need the skills. Keep learning, keep refining. One day, you'll build something like this, and it won't just be pretty. It'll be perfect." Antoine's chest swelled with renewed purpose. "I will, monsieur. I promise." Bailly motioned with a rare smile, tugging at the corners of his mouth. "Good. Now get some food and go rest. You can't build an empire on an empty stomach and no sleep."

Voiceover (Older Antoine): *"Bailly's words stayed with me long after I left his bakery. He saw the flaws in my work, but he also saw the potential. In those early days, he taught me to embrace failure as a teacher and perfection as a journey, not a destination."*

Antoine's skills flourished. Bailly's relentless mentorship, though tough, pushed him to new heights. He learned to master the perfect croissant, its layers as delicate as parchment. He conquered the soufflé, timing its rise with the precision of a clockmaker. And slowly but surely, he began to experiment with sugar.

One evening, long after the bakery had closed, Antoine stood over a bubbling pot of molten sugar. The golden liquid swirled and shimmered, its heat radiating against his flushed cheeks. He dipped a spoon into the mixture and carefully drizzled it onto a marble slab, creating delicate, lace-like patterns. When the sugar cooled, he lifted the fragile pieces, holding them up to the light; they sparkled like the finest jewels. Bailly entered the kitchen, his eyebrows shooting up at the sight. "And what's this?" "A new idea," Antoine said, a nervous but proud smile on his face. "For decorations." Bailly picked up one of the sugar pieces, turning it over in his thick fingers. He bit off a corner, chewing thoughtfully before nodding. "Not bad. But if you're going to experiment, don't waste my sugar. Use scraps next time." Antoine grinned. "Yes, monsieur." The baker's lips curled with the hint of yet another smile. "You've got the spark, boy. Just be sure you don't burn out before your flames have touched everything they must." Bailey had a habit of offering the same lesson—or warning—each time he reviewed my work.

Antoine's mind raced as he worked into the night, refining his sugar work and dreaming of the day his creations would grace the tables of kings. He didn't know when or how, but he was certain of one thing: he would be remembered as one of the greats. His intense devotion to his craft overflowed from the very beginning.

CHAPTER 3
THE TURNING POINT

The months had now turned into a year at Bailly's bakery, and Antoine Carême's confidence grew with each passing day. Yet, with every task he mastered, he found himself yearning for more. The bread was essential, and pastries were elegant, but Antoine's heart lay in something larger—something extraordinary. He wanted to fashion pieces that would make people stop and marvel, that would linger in their minds long after the last crumb had disappeared.

The sun cast a pale golden hue over Paris as Antoine approached Bailly's bakery, his heart beating harder than the heels of his worn boots against the cobblestones. He carried a bundle of parchment sketches in his hands, each more intricate than the last. Today, he had to show them to Bailly. If the baker's sternness softened even faintly, Antoine would know he was on the right path.

The scent of fresh baguettes and caramelized sugar inside the bakery wrapped around him like a comforting embrace. The apprentices bustled about, their chatter blending with the rhythmic hum of kneading and whisking. But Antoine focused completely on Bailly, who stood at the back, scrutinizing a tray of pastries as if they held the universe's secrets. "Monsieur Bailly," Antoine said, his voice steady but tight with anticipation.

Bailly looked up, his eyes contracting as he wiped his hands on his flour-streaked apron. "What is it, Carême?" Antoine hesitated, then held out the bundle of sketches. "I've been working on these drawings for pièces montées. I thought you might... look at them." Bailly took the papers, his expression unreadable. He spread them out on the counter, his fingers tracing the delicate lines. Antoine held his breath as Bailly stood over the towering temple made of spun sugar, its base supported by intricate pastry columns. "Ambitious," Bailly muttered, echoing the word he'd used months ago. He tapped a finger against one sketch. "This one, a dome of sugar atop a lattice base—it could collapse under its own weight if the sugar isn't tempered just right. And these pillars? They'll crack if your dough is too dry." Antoine's stomach sank as he spoke, "I can fix those things, monsieur. I just need time to practice." Bailly's expression, showing a hint of a smile. "Practice, yes. But you'll also need discipline and patience. Vision alone won't build these." He gathered the sketches and handed them back. "Keep refining. You're on the right track, Carême. Don't get discouraged." Relief and resolve surged through Antoine. He carefully tucked the sketches back into his satchel. "Merci, monsieur. I won't let you down."

Voiceover (Older Antoine): *"That moment, standing in Bailly's bakery with my sketches clutched in my hands, was a turning point. His voice wasn't that of praise, but it was fuel. I saw the path in front of me with clarity."*

The weeks that followed were a blur of experimentation. By day, Antoine honed his skills under Bailly's watchful eye, perfecting the basics. By night, he transformed the bakery's workbench into his own laboratory. He boiled sugar until it gleamed like molten gold, shaping it into delicate spirals and lattices. He tested dough after dough, searching for the perfect balance of elasticity and strength.

One evening, as the other apprentices prepared to leave, Bailly stopped Antoine with a hand on his shoulder. "Stay a moment, Carême," Bailly said, his tone stern but not unkind. Antoine set down the tray he had been cleaning, his brow furrowed. "Yes, monsieur?" Bailly gestured toward a stack of ingredients on the counter: flour, eggs, sugar, almonds, and fresh lemons. "I want to see what you can do. Make something. Anything. But it has to be yours. No recipes, no instructions. Just your instincts." Antoine quickly tied his apron tighter around his waist. "Merci, monsieur. I won't disappoint you." Bailly crossed his arms and leaned against the wall, watching as Antoine set to work. The kitchen, usually filled with noise and motion, was now silent save for the soft sounds of Antoine's preparations. He sifted flour, cracked eggs with a practiced flick of his wrist, and whipped sugar and lemon zest into a fragrant cream.

As the hours passed, the counter transformed into a canvas. Antoine fashioned a tart with a golden pâte sucrée base, filled with almond cream, and topped with thinly sliced lemons arranged in a sunburst pattern. To finish, he spun sugar into delicate strands, draping them over the tart like a gossamer veil. When he finally stepped back, his hands trembling with exhaustion, Bailly approached the counter. The older man examined the tart from every angle, his face impassive. He picked up a knife and cut a small slice, tasting it slowly. Antoine held his breath.

"The dough is crisp, the cream smooth, the sugar work... delicate," Bailly said at last. His gaze met Antoine's, and there was a glimmer of pride in his demeanor, which was first for Bailly. "It's good, Carême. Very good."

"Thank you, monsieur." Bailly set down the knife. "You've come a long way, boy. But don't think this is the end. It's just the beginning."

The following morning was a crisp one; Bailly handed Antoine a task that would push him closer to his goal. The bakery had received an order from a wealthy merchant who wanted a dessert centerpiece for his daughter's wedding. The request was unusual; the customer wanted something "grand and unforgettable." Bailly, while skeptical of such extravagance, saw an opportunity to test Antoine's growing skills; Antoine began to see that Bailey was showing some faith and trust in his apprentice. "Show me your craft, Le Petit Architecte," Bailly said, voice rough yet expectant. "Design something fit for a celebration, but don't get carried away. Keep it practical."

Antoine's pulse quickened. He hurried to the back of the bakery, where he laid out his parchment and began to sketch. He envisioned a tower of pâte à choux, carefully arranged and bound together with delicate strands of caramel. Around the base, he planned to add sugared almonds and candied flowers, creating a cascade of colors and textures.

Over the next few days, Antoine threw himself into the project. He practiced piping the choux pastry until each piece was identical in size. He learned to spin sugar, carefully forming golden threads that shimmered like sunlight. The other apprentices watched him with a mix of awe and skepticism, their muttered comments trailing behind him as he moved about the bakery.

The night before the wedding, Antoine assembled the pièce montée. With steady hands, he stacked the choux pastries into a towering cone, securing them with caramel that hardened into a glossy, amber shell. He added the sugared almonds and flowers, each placement precise and deliberate. When he stepped back to admire his work, his demeanor was prideful. Bailly approached, his expression unreadable. He circled the centerpiece, while he checked every detail. "Well?" Antoine asked, unable to hide the nervous edge in his voice. Bailly grunted. "It's...impressive. But details matter. Fix these flowers and balance the caramel better next time." The merchant arrived the next morning and was stunned by the centerpiece. As the pièce montée left the bakery, Antoine stood in the doorway, feeling the weight of possibility; he knew this was only his induction.

Voiceover (Older Antoine): *"That first centerpiece was the beginning of everything. Bailly gave me the tools, but it was up to me to build the dream."*

CHAPTER 3A
INNER THOUGHTS

Antoine stood alone in the bakery's quiet after the pièce montée had been carried away, the lingering scent of caramel and toasted almonds mingling with the faint smokiness of the ovens. He wiped his hands on his apron, staring at the now-empty workbench where hours of painstaking effort had taken shape. The applause from the merchant's visit echoed faintly in his mind, but it didn't settle his unease.

Inner Monologue (Antoine):

"Success should feel sweeter than this. My pièce montée impressed them, yet all I see are its flaws—the sugar that set too fast, the flowers that leaned a fraction off balance. Bailly saw them, too, of course. But his critiques don't sting anymore. I see my own failures before he does. The question is… will I ever stop chasing perfection?" Or is this drive—to see beauty, to craft it—destined to be a hunger that's never truly sated? Maybe that's what it means to have too many aspirations. Not a destination, but a constant pull forward."

Antoine peered over to the bundle of sketches peeking out from his satchel. He pulled them out and leafed through them, his fingers lingering on the sketches Bailly had critiqued only weeks before. Each line and curve seemed to taunt him now, whispering of a vision still out of reach.

Inner Monologue (Antoine):

"When I look at these sketches, I see more than just ideas. I see a future—a way to transform pastry into art, to make the world stop and marvel at what's possible. But I'm not there yet. Not even close."

Every success feels like the edge of a new challenge. I thought that once I impressed Bailly, once I proved myself, it would get easier. But all it's done is show me how much more there is to learn and how far I still have to go. And yet... I wouldn't trade this feeling for anything. The thrill of creation, the quiet hours spent shaping something extraordinary from the simplest ingredients—it's where I feel most alive. Someday, these designs won't just live on parchment. They'll stand tall in banquet halls, admired by commoners, emperors, and kings alike. But for now, I'll keep working. I'll keep refining. Because the dream isn't just to create something unforgettable—it's to become someone unforgettable."

Antoine tucked the sketches back into his bag and turned to the darkened kitchen. The tools of his trade—rolling pins, molds, piping bags—gleamed faintly in the dim light. He reached out, brushing his fingers against the smooth wood of a rolling pin, his tenacity solidifying with every breath.

Inner Monologue (Antoine):

"Tonight, I will rest. But tomorrow? Tomorrow, I will knead, shape, and build with more precision than ever before. Because one day, this hunger, this fire—it won't just be mine. It'll be something everyone can taste and see, something they'll remember long after I'm gone."

Antoine extinguished the last of the candles and stepped out into the cool Parisian night, his thoughts full of both restlessness and hope. Somewhere in the city, dreams as bold as he was being born. But Antoine Carême didn't just dream—he worked, created, and believed that one day, we would see his vision as clearly as he did.

CHAPTER 4
THE INVITATION

The bakery whirred with its usual rhythm, but Antoine felt poised on the edge of transformation. Days had turned to weeks and weeks into months since his lemon tart and first wedding centerpiece had earned Bailly's rare praise, and though the apprentices treated him with a newfound respect, Antoine's thoughts were consumed by the possibilities ahead. His sketches had grown more ambitious, his nights longer as he experimented with towering sugar creations that glittered like crystal in the faint candlelight.

Yet, even with this progress, a discomfort lingered. Antoine couldn't shake the sense that the bakery—for all its warmth and familiarity—had become too small for the vision he carried. He longed for a stage grand enough to match his hopes, though he dared not voice such thoughts aloud.

It was during one such evening, as Antoine worked into the night shaping a miniature bridge of caramelized sugar, that the bell above the bakery door jingled. He froze, the delicate structure in his hands trembling as heavy footsteps echoed through the quiet shop.

"Who's there?" Antoine called, his voice wary but steady.

A man stepped into the warm glow of the kitchen. He was tall and impeccably dressed, his coat tailored from fine wool and his boots polished to a mirror sheen. His acute eyesight swept over the room, lingering briefly on the sugar bridge before settling on Antoine.

"Are you Antoine Carême?" the man asked, his voice smooth and authoritative.

Antoine wiped his hands on his apron, "Oui, monsieur. How can I help you?"

The man produced a sealed letter from his coat and held it out. "I come on behalf of Charles-Maurice de Talleyrand-Périgord. His Excellency requests your presence at his estate."

Antoine stared at the letter, his breathing rate increasing, Talleyrand. The name was spoken with reverence and intrigue in every corner of Paris. A diplomat, a powerbroker, a man whose influence extended from Napoleon's court to the farthest reaches of Europe. What could such a figure want with an unassuming baker's apprentice?

"Me?" Antoine managed, his voice barely above a whisper.

"You have impressed more than just your master, young man. Talleyrand has heard of your skill and wishes to see it for himself. Be at the Château de Valençay tomorrow morning."

He placed the letter on the counter and turned to leave, his boots clicking against the floorboards. Antoine watched him go, the letter untouched until the door had closed and silence enveloped the room once more.

With trembling fingers, Antoine broke the seal and unfolded the parchment. The handwriting was elegant, each line carefully laid out. The letter was brief but clear: an invitation to present his culinary creations to Talleyrand himself.

Voiceover (Older Antoine): *"That letter was both a beacon and a burden. To be summoned by a man of Talleyrand's stature was a hope that was unimaginable, yet it was also terrifying. This was no longer about impressing Bailly or perfecting a single tart. This was the threshold of something far greater."*

The next morning, Antoine hesitated before entering the bakery, the letter clutched in his hand. Bailly stood behind the counter, kneading dough with his usual vigor. When Antoine cleared his throat, Bailly glanced up, his brow contracting at the sight of the parchment.

"What is it, boy?" Bailly asked, wiping his hands on his apron.

Antoine stepped forward and held out the letter. "It's from Talleyrand. He… he wants me to present my work to him."

Bailly's expression remained unreadable as he took the letter and scanned its contents. After a long moment, he grunted and handed it back. "Talleyrand's no fool. If he's called for you, it's because he sees something worth testing. Don't disappoint him—or me."

Antoine's swelled with pride and apprehension. "Thank you, monsieur. For everything."

Bailly spoke with supportive words, though his tone remained surly. "You've come a long way, Antoine. But remember, ambition's a good thing, so long as it doesn't blind you. Now go on. You've got work to do."

Sleep eluded Antoine that night. His mind raced with questions and anxieties. What should he prepare? What if he failed? As dawn broke, painting the city in hues of gold and rose, Antoine approached the challenge as he always had, with a relentless belief in his trade.

He spent the morning selecting ingredients with care. Fine flour, fresh cream, sugar as white as snow. From Bailly's stores, he borrowed molds and tools, ensuring everything was perfect. His hands moved with precision, a pièce montée that reflected his vision: a towering confection adorned with delicate sugar swans gliding across a caramel lake, its base sturdy and spires reaching for the heavens.

By the time the carriage arrived to take him to the château, Antoine stood ready, his creation secured in a wooden crate lined with straw. He adjusted his apron, smoothed his hair, and stepped outside, where the driver waited with a curious glance.

"Are you ready, young man?" the driver asked, helping Antoine lift the crate onto the carriage.

Antoine hesitated for a moment, "As ready as I'll ever be."

As Antoine wiped his hands on his apron for the last time, he paused at the threshold of Bailly's bakery. The warmth of the ovens seemed to call him back, but whispers of grander things echoed in his ears. He stepped into the streets of Paris, where destiny and danger awaited.

Bailey stood in his flour-dusted apron, gazing out the window at Antoine. His face showed no emotion save for the faint glint of a single tear.

I could see him. I wanted to turn back, to thank him for everything he had done for me. But I knew he wasn't the kind of man who needed words. Deep in my heart, I understood—that the greatest way to honor and truly thank him was to succeed. To be the best.

The journey to Valençay felt both interminable and fleeting. The rolling countryside blurred past the carriage windows, each passing mile bringing Antoine closer to a destiny he couldn't yet comprehend. When the château came into view, its grandeur took his breath away. It rose from the landscape like a vision, its ornate facade gleaming in the afternoon sun.

Antoine stepped out of the carriage, clutching the crate as if it contained his very soul. A steward met him at the entrance, his expression neutral but polite.

"Follow me," the steward said, leading Antoine through the labyrinthine halls of the estate. The air was thick with opulence, from the gilded mirrors that lined the walls to the plush carpets that muffled their footsteps. Finally, they arrived at a set of double doors.

The steward knocked once and pushed them open, revealing a grand dining hall. At its center sat Charles-Maurice de Talleyrand, a man whose presence filled the room despite his seated position. Antoine could see Talleyrand appraising him as he entered, and for a moment, the boy felt as though he were being weighed and measured.

"Monsieur Carême," Talleyrand said, his voice cultured and smooth. "Welcome. I trust your journey was pleasant?"

Antoine bowed deeply, his hands gripping the crate. "Oui, Monseigneur. Thank you for inviting me."

Talleyrand gestured to a long table. "Show me what you've brought."

With great care, Antoine set the crate on the table and began to unpack his pièce montée. The room seemed to hold its breath as he revealed the creation, its delicate features gleaming under the chandeliers. Antoine stepped back, his heart once again hammering inside as Talleyrand rose from his chair.

The diplomat circled the confection slowly, his hands clasped behind his back. "Exquisite," he murmured, pausing to observe the sugar swans. "You have an artist's touch, Monsieur Carême. Tell me, what drives you to form such beauty?"

Antoine hesitated, "To bring joy, Monseigneur. To show that even in the simplest ingredients, there is the potential for greatness."

"A noble answer. And one that suits my table well. You will remain here, Monsieur Carême. I have need of your talents."

Antoine's breath caught. "You mean... to work for you?"

Talleyrand nodded. "Precisely. Your journey is just beginning, young man. Welcome to my kitchen."

Voiceover (Older Antoine): *"That day marked the start of a new chapter, one that would take me from the streets of Paris to the courts of kings. I had crossed the threshold, but I had no idea of the challenges that lay ahead. Talleyrand's kitchen was not merely a place of creation; it was a crucible where skill and endurance were tested at every turn. And I was ready to face it all."*

PART II
THE CHEF OF KINGS

CHAPTER 5
INTO TALLEYRAND'S KITCHEN – THE FIRST TEST

Paris awaited, its streets alive with opportunity and peril. Antoine's sketches and dreams were all he carried, but they were enough. Antoine Carême stood at the threshold of Talleyrand's grand kitchen, his breath catching as he took in the scene before him. The scent of simmering sauces and roasting meats hit Antoine the moment he stepped inside, richer and more intoxicating than the warm, yeasted air of Bailly's bakery. Here, copper pots gleamed under candlelight, flames licked hungrily at blackened cast iron, and the symphony of chopping, whisking, and shouted orders filled the cavernous space. Cooks and assistants darted back and forth, their movements precise and purposeful. This was no ordinary kitchen; it was an empire of culinary mastery.

For a moment, Antoine felt overwhelmed, his confidence faltering as he absorbed the scale of his new surroundings. The weight of expectation settled heavily on his shoulders, but he quickly reminded himself why he was there. He had earned this opportunity and would prove himself worthy of it.

Voiceover (Older Antoine): *"I had thought Bailly's bakery was the pinnacle of discipline and precision, but Talleyrand's kitchen was something else entirely. It was not merely a place to create—it was a battlefield where only the strongest and most skilled could survive. And in that moment, I realized that I was starting from the bottom once again."*

"Carême!" a sharp voice barked, cutting through the din. Antoine turned to see a tall, imposing man striding toward him, his chef's whites immaculate despite the chaos around him. His tone biting, "I am Dupont, head chef of His Excellency's kitchen. You will answer to me."

"Oui, Chef Dupont. It is an honor." Standing tall, Dupont watched the apprentices intently, always assessing look watching their every move.

"We shall see if you can survive here, boy. Talleyrand demands perfection, and I have no patience for anything less. Move quickly or move out. We have no place for slow hands in His Excellency's kitchen. "Your first task is simple: prepare a dessert for tonight's dinner. A hundred guests. You have three hours. Impress me, or pack your bags."

Antoine's heart thundered, "Yes, Chef."

Dupont gestured to an empty workstation, then turned and barked orders at another assistant. Antoine exhaled slowly and approached the station, his mentality in a state of flux. The ingredients laid out before him were plentiful: eggs, sugar, cream, almonds, chocolate, fresh berries. He closed his eyes for a moment, picturing the designs he had sketched late into the night back at Bailly's bakery. This was his chance to prove himself, and failure was not an option.

Voiceover (Older Antoine): *"In those first moments, standing in Talleyrand's kitchen, I felt the weight of expectation like never before. But beneath the fear, there was a spark of determination. This was the test I had been preparing for all my life, though I didn't yet realize it."*

Antoine set to work, his hands moving with practiced precision. He decided on a delicate raspberry tart, its flavors simple yet elegant. The base would be a crisp pâte sucrée, filled with almond cream and topped with fresh raspberries glazed in apricot preserves. To elevate the dish, he planned to adorn it with a lattice of spun sugar as fine and intricate as lace.

He worked methodically, tuning out the cacophony around him. Flour dusted the countertop as he rolled out the dough, his movements steady despite the tremor of nerves in his chest. The almond cream came together smoothly, its nutty aroma mingling with the sweetness of the berries he carefully selected and arranged.

As the tart baked, Antoine turned his attention to the sugar. The syrup bubbled and hissed in the copper pot as he heated it to the perfect temperature. He dipped a fork into the molten sugar, then flicked it back and forth over a marble slab, creating delicate threads that hardened into a golden lattice. By the time the tart was ready, Antoine's station was immaculate, his creation gleaming on a silver platter. He stepped back and wiped his hands as Dupont approached.

Dupont eyed the tart. He circled it like a predator, his fingers hovering over the spun sugar lattice before breaking off a piece. Dupont tasted the tart in silence, his expression unreadable. Finally, he set the fork down and looked at Antoine. "The pâte sucrée is crisp, the almond cream smooth, the raspberries fresh. The sugar work… precise." He paused, "It is acceptable."

Relief flooded Antoine, but he kept his expression neutral. "Thank you, Chef Dupont." Dupont's lips twitched in what might have been a smile. "You've earned your place, for now, Carême. But remember, this is only the beginning. flawlessness is expected every time." "I understand, Chef."

That evening, Antoine stood at the edge of the dining hall, watching from the shadows as the guests sampled his tart. Laughter and conversation filled the air, and he saw more than one nobleman gesture with admiration toward the dessert. Talleyrand himself tasted a piece, his expression giving nothing away though he inclined his head slightly in Dupont's direction.

Voiceover (Older Antoine): *"I did not receive praise that night but did not need it. The empty plates and satisfied smiles were enough to tell me that I had succeeded. For the first time, I felt the quiet satisfaction of meeting a challenge head-on and emerging victorious."*

The days that followed were tough. Dupont's kitchen was a crucible of discipline, and Antoine faced countless tests, each more demanding than the last. He made mistakes, and Dupont's snappish tongue spared him no mercy. The other cooks were equally unsparing, their camaraderie tempered by competition. Yet, with every critique came a lesson, and with every lesson, Antoine grew stronger. As Antoine cleaned his station, Dupont approached him. The kitchen was quiet, the fires banked low. "Carême," Dupont said, his tone softer than usual. "You have talent, but talent is not enough. Only discipline will ensure you do not fall." Antoine gestured. "I will not fail or disappoint you, Chef."

Dupont studied him for a moment, "See that you don't."

As Dupont walked away, Antoine turned back to his work, his mind clear and firm more than ever. He was no longer just an apprentice or a dreamer. He was a part of Talleyrand's kitchen and would prove himself worthy of the name.

Voiceover (Older Antoine): *"Those first weeks in Talleyrand's kitchen forged me like steel in a fire. The lessons were harsh, the demands relentless, but they prepared me for the challenges yet to come. I had entered the crucible, and though I did not know it then, I was being shaped into something greater."*

CHAPTER 6
RISING TENSIONS

The days in Talleyrand's kitchen settled into a grueling routine, each one more challenging than the last. Dupont's standards were exacting, and Antoine found himself constantly under the head chef's watchful eye. The atmosphere in the kitchen was a blend of camaraderie and competition; every cook knew that a single mistake could mean their dismissal, but every success brought a flicker of pride to the team.

For Antoine, those days were a crucible of transformation. His hands, once soft and unsteady, became firm and confident. He learned to read the subtle signs of a custard's perfect set or the precise moment when sugar turned from caramel to ash. Yet, no matter how much he improved, Dupont's critiques were relentless.

"Too much glaze on the pastries. They'll slide off the plate," Dupont snapped one morning as Antoine presented a tray of éclairs.

Antoine's jaw tightened, "I'll fix it, Chef."

As he returned to his station, one of the cooks leaned in. Jacques, a broad-shouldered man with an easy grin, gave him a conspiratorial wink. "Don't let Dupont get to you, Carême. He yells at all of us. It's how he says 'good morning.'"

Antoine allowed himself a small smile. "Then he must like me more than most. He never stops yelling at me."

Jacques chuckled, clapping Antoine on the back. "That means he sees potential. Keep your head down and your hands moving. You'll outlast the lot of us."

Voiceover (Older Antoine): *"Dupont's kitchen was a battlefield, but not all were enemies. I found comrades among the heat and fire—dreamers, pragmatists, men who understood that perfection was both our torment and salvation."*

One storm, however, was brewing outside the kitchen. The politics surrounding Talleyrand's estate were rife with intrigue, and whispers of upheaval reached even the bustling heart of the kitchen. Rumors of Napoleon's tensions within the court filled the servants' quarters, and the weight of expectation trickled down to the kitchen staff.

One evening, as Antoine cleaned his station, he overheard two servants whispering by the doorway.

"Have you heard? There's talk of Napoleon's next campaign—his greed grows by the day."

"And Talleyrand? What role will he play?"

Antoine pretended not to listen; the kitchen might have seemed removed from the grand machinations of politics, but Antoine knew better. Every dish that left their counters reflected Talleyrand's power and influence.

As Dupont observed Antoine's work one evening, his expression was unusually contemplative. "Carême," he said, his voice low. "The world beyond this kitchen is watching. Do not forget that every dish you create reflects more than just yourself. You are shaping His Excellency's reputation—and your own." The weight of what Dupont said was settling over him. "I understand, Chef. I won't fail."

Dupont's mouth contracted in what might have been approval, but his sharp tone returned as he pointed to Antoine's station. "Then clean that mess before it becomes a disaster."

The Chef of Kings, The King of Chefs

The amity in the kitchen was often tested by the high stakes, but moments of levity broke through the tension. One afternoon, Jacques challenged Antoine to a race to peel and dice a tray of apples. Laughter bubbled up as Antoine, though quick and precise, found himself falling behind Jacques' lumbering but surprisingly efficient pace.

"You'll have to do better than that to beat me, Carême!" Jacques teased, tossing a perfectly diced apple cube onto Antoine's tray.

Antoine smirked. "You might win the race, but my cuts are cleaner. That's what Dupont will notice."

The other cooks, watching from nearby stations, chimed in with their own playful jabs, and the weight of their work lifted for a moment. These small moments of connection kept Antoine grounded amid the relentless pressure.

That evening, Dupont summoned Antoine to his office. The head chef's private space was a stark contrast to the chaos of the kitchen, its shelves lined with meticulously labeled jars and a single ledger resting on the desk.

"Carême," Dupont began, his tone unusually grave. "His Excellency has requested a menu for an upcoming banquet. Important guests will be present, and the meal must reflect not only his wealth but his taste. He has asked that you make one of the centerpieces." Antoine's eyes widened. "Me, Chef?"

Dupont with nerve-racking words. "Do not mistake this for an honor. It is a test. If you fail, it will reflect on me as much as on you. Can you handle it?"

Antoine straightened his back. "I can, Chef."

Dupont studied him for a long moment before gesturing to the ledger. "You will find the specifications here. Talleyrand has requested something… theatrical. He wishes to make an impression. Start tomorrow morning."

Antoine left the office with the ledger in hand; he flipped through the pages filled with notes on past menus and lavish banquets, and the enormity of the task began to sink in. This wasn't just about food; it was about politics, power, and prestige. His creation would be more than a dish—it would be a statement.

Voiceover (Older Antoine): *"That assignment was the first time I understood the true weight of my art. In Talleyrand's circle, food was not just sustenance. It was diplomacy, a tool to sway hearts and minds. The stakes were higher than I had ever imagined."*

The next morning, Antoine began work on his pièce montée. He began to sketch once his work was finished, envisioning a towering creation inspired by the gardens of Versailles. It would feature delicate arches of nougatine, columns of spun sugar, and tiers of petits fours arranged like blooming flowers. Every detail had to be perfect.

The kitchen hummed with its usual routine, but Antoine's station became its own little universe. Jacques occasionally glanced over, offering encouragement, while Dupont loomed in the background, his presence both a comfort and a pressure.

Antoine's first attempt ended in disaster. The sugar columns cracked under the weight of the nougatine arches, and one of the tiers collapsed in a sticky mess. Frustration boiled within him, but he forced himself to start again. He adjusted the ratios of sugar to water, strengthened the base, and reshaped the arches.

By the third day, the pièce montée began to take shape. Its golden hues shimmered under the kitchen's lantern light, and the delicate aroma of almonds and caramel filled the air. Antoine stepped back, his hands trembling from exhaustion, but his heart swelled with pride.

Dupont approached, his expression unreadable as he studied the creation, then ran a finger along the edge of a nougatine arch, "It will do. Prepare it for transport." Not words he enjoyed hearing or ones that imparted confidence. Antoine exhaled a shaky breath. "Yes, Chef."

The banquet was a spectacle of opulence. Chandeliers cast a warm glow over the dining hall, where nobles and diplomats dined on courses that reflected Talleyrand's taste for extravagance. When Antoine's pièce montée was unveiled, a hush fell over the room. The golden arches and sugar columns caught the light like jewels, and murmurs of admiration rippled through the crowd.

From his place in the shadows, Antoine watched as Talleyrand himself examined the centerpiece. The diplomat's expression remained inscrutable, but he turned to Dupont and nodded once. An immediate sigh of relief came over Antoine.

Voiceover (Older Antoine): *"That night, I saw how my work could move people. It was not the applause or the admiration that stayed with me but the knowledge that I had risen to the challenge. It was a small victory, but it lit an inferno that would be my driving force for years to come."*

As the guests departed and the dining hall emptied, Dupont approached Antoine in the quiet kitchen.

"You did well," Dupont said simply. "But remember, Carême, the higher you climb, the further you have to fall. Stay hungry."

Antoine's expression of exhaustion gave way to a quiet resolve. "I will, Chef."

The night marked a turning point. Antoine was no longer just another cook in Talleyrand's kitchen. He was carving a place for himself, one masterpiece at a time.

CHAPTER 7
AMBITION'S SHADOW

The days following the Palais-Royal gala passed in a whirlwind of speculation. Antoine Carême's pièce montée became the talk of Paris, its elegance and grandeur whispered about in salons and drawing rooms. Invitations from nobles and merchants flooded Talleyrand's estate, each requesting Antoine for their own events. The young chef had become a rising star, but with fame came new responsibilities and dangers.

Talleyrand summoned Antoine to his study one crisp morning. The room was bathed in sunlight, its walls lined with books and maps that hinted at the diplomat's far-reaching influence. Antoine approached the desk, his nerves taut.

"Carême," Talleyrand began, his tone measured. "You have brought great acclaim to my household. Your work has not gone unnoticed, but I must warn you—success in this city attracts both admirers and rivals."

Antoine inclined his head. "I understand, Monseigneur. I will do my best to uphold the reputation of your kitchen."

Talleyrand's studied him. "Good. Your next commission will test not only your skill but your discretion. A prominent figure from Napoleon's court has requested your services. You will prepare a banquet at their residence, one that reflects the grandeur of France. Dupont will oversee the logistics, but the creative vision is yours."

For Antoine, this was an opportunity of unprecedented scale, but it also carried immense risk. Any misstep could have consequences far beyond the kitchen.

"I will not fail, Monseigneur," Antoine said with a calmness.

Voiceover (Older Antoine): *"Working for Talleyrand had taught me that food was more than sustenance—it was a language, a tool of influence. This commission, however, brought the lessons into sharper focus. It was not merely a test of my skill; it was a balancing act on a knife's edge."*

Preparations for the banquet began immediately. Antoine dove into his work, drafting elaborate sculptures and refining his techniques. The menu was a delicate balance of traditional French flavors and innovative presentation, featuring dishes that showcased the finest ingredients Paris had to offer. Jacques, ever the loyal friend, watched with a mix of admiration and concern. "You're working yourself into the ground, Carême," he said one evening as they cleaned their stations. "Even you need sleep." Antoine shook his head, his eyes bright. "There's too much at stake, Jacques. If I succeed, this could open doors I never imagined." Jacques sighed but said nothing more, knowing his friend's stubbornness well.

The day of the banquet arrived, and Antoine led a small team to the stately residence of General Moreau, one of Napoleon's trusted allies. The kitchen was a flurry of activity as they unloaded crates of ingredients and equipment. Antoine directed the team, his voice calm but firm.

The pièce montée for this event was a triumph of engineering: a towering sugar sculpture of an eagle in flight, wings outstretched over a base of marzipan roses and candied violets. It symbolized strength and beauty, a subtle nod to the grandeur of Napoleon's empire. As the dishes were plated and the pièce montée unveiled in the grand dining hall, Antoine watched from the shadows. The guests murmured their approval, their faces alight with admiration. General Moreau himself approached the sculpture, examining it with a critical eye before a nod of satisfaction.

"You have outdone yourself," Moreau declared, his voice carrying across the room. "This is a testament to your genius." Antoine allowed himself a small smile, his chest swelling with gratification.

Voiceover (Older Antoine): *"As the banquet unfolded, I saw it clearly—this was no longer about sugar and flour. This was influence, power, and art. My work didn't just satisfy appetites; it shaped reputations."*

Antoine's pièce montée at the Palais-Royal had cemented his reputation, but with fame came scrutiny. Among the murmurs of admiration, there were whispers of resentment. At first, the looks were fleeting, an extra second of observation from across the workstations, subtle glances when he passed. Then came the "accidents"—a missing tool, salt swapped for sugar, a crucial ingredient conveniently misplaced. Antoine ignored them, focusing on his work. But one evening, as he reached for his notes, a small parchment lay in their place. No name. Just the warning, scrawled in neat, deliberate script:

"Beware the price of ambition."

He turned sharply, but the kitchen was empty. A cold unease settled over him; this was no mere competition. Someone wanted him to know they were watching.

Antoine felt the weight of the words. Had he made an enemy?

In the days that followed, he worked harder than ever, determined not to be rattled. But the tension in the air was undeniable. Some cooks muttered as he passed. Others stopped speaking when he entered the room. And unseen figures watched his every move in the shadows of Talleyrand's court. Requests kept streaming in, each more elaborate than the last. A duchess desired an edible replica of her summer estate. A visiting ambassador wanted a dessert that symbolized peace between nations. Each project was a test not only of Antoine's skill but of his endurance. Despite his growing reputation, whispers of jealousy began to circulate within the kitchen. Some other cooks, emboldened by their frustrations, grumbled openly about Antoine's rapid ascent. "He's barely out of Bailly's bakery," one muttered. "And now he acts as though he owns the kitchen."

Jacques confronted Antoine one evening, his usually easy demeanor tinged with concern. Watch yourself, Carême," Jacques uttered with his voice low. "There are those who do not take kindly to another man's rise."

Antoine frowned, "I've done nothing but work hard, and I've been warned countless times; I do realize what my success is bringing, both good and bad. I am prepared." Jacques sighed. "That's exactly the problem. Hard work makes you a target in a place like this. Just… watch your back."

The tension reached a boiling point during preparations for another high-profile event. As Antoine worked on a delicate sugar structure, he noticed one of his molds missing from its usual place. Panic shot through him as he scanned the room, finally spotting the mold in the hands of another cook. "What are you doing with that?" Antoine demanded, his voice sharper than intended. The cook shrugged, a smirk playing on his lips. "Borrowing it. Is that a problem, Chef Carême?" Antoine's hands tightened into fists but forced himself to remain calm. "Return it when you're finished. Some of us have deadlines to meet."

The exchange drew the attention of Dupont, who strode over, his expression stormy. "What's going on here?"

Antoine took a deep breath, steadying himself. "Nothing, Chef. Just a misunderstanding." Dupont focuses on Antoine, but he says nothing further, moving on to inspect another station. Antoine returned to his work, the incident leaving a sour taste in his mouth. The following evening, another note was slipped under Antoine's door. This one read:

Your determination will destroy you.

Antoine once again looked at a written warning, his chest tightening. The shadows seemed to grow longer, the walls of his small quarters pressing closer. Was this a warning? A threat? He couldn't shake the feeling that someone was watching, waiting for him to falter. Despite the growing unease, Antoine refused to slow down. The commission for the ambassador's banquet consumed his every waking hour. It was ambitious: a pièce montée depicting a dove mid-flight, surrounded by cascading sugar ribbons and marzipan olive branches. Every detail had to be flawless. That night, as Antoine worked alone, he heard a faint rustling behind him. He turned sharply, his heart racing, but the kitchen was empty. His eyes darted to the shadows, searching for movement, but there was nothing. Shaking his head, he returned to his work, though the apprehension remained. Antoine knew one thing: he had to confront and conquer his fears, just as he had done countless times to reach this point in his life.

The following evening was the banquet, and it was another feat. The dove centerpiece drew gasps of admiration, and the ambassador himself declared it a masterpiece. Antoine accepted the praise with quiet humility, but the weight of the anonymous warnings hung heavy over him.

As the banquet concluded, Dupont approached Antoine in the quiet kitchen. His usual stern demeanor was softened by a rare flicker of concern. "Carême," Dupont said. "Take care, Antoine, always remember that the higher you climb, the more enemies you make." Immense fortitude simmering inside. "I won't let them stop me, Chef." Dupont studied him for a moment before nodding. "Learn to stay grounded, no matter the accolades your work earns, or life will become a burden. Don't let your desires consume you."

Voiceover (Older Antoine): *"I began to understand the double-edged nature of my culinary dreams. It was my driving force, but it also made me a target. The whispers, warnings, and shadows were all part of the price I paid to pursue greatness."*

As Antoine stepped into the cool night air, he looked up at the stars, their light sharp and distant. His path was illuminated, but it was also fraught with unseen dangers. And yet, he knew he could not turn back.

CHAPTER 8
SHADOWS AND SECRETS

The cryptic note had planted a seed of anxiety in Antoine's mind, not something easily ignored, but he buried the discomfort beneath his relentless drive. His days were consumed by commissions, each one more elaborate than the last, and his nights were filled with restless dreams. The price of success, he reminded himself, was the willingness to shoulder its burdens.

The whispers of jealousy and rivalry within Paris's culinary circles grew louder. Dupont's warning echoed in Antoine's thoughts as he noticed subtle changes in the people around him. Rivals, who once voiced their criticisms without hesitation, now delivered veiled compliments, their words carefully chosen and their smiles lacking genuine warmth. Among his fellow cooks, the camaraderie of shared craft was shadowed by an undercurrent of tension, simmering quietly like an unwatched pot on the edge of boiling over. One evening, Jacques approached Antoine as they cleaned their stations. His usual jovial demeanor was tinged with concern.

"Carême, have you noticed anything... strange lately?" Jacques asked, his voice low. Antoine glanced at him, setting down his knife. "Strange how?" Jacques hesitated, wiping his hands on his apron. "There are rumors. People say you've made enemies. Powerful ones." Antoine forced a smile. "Jacques, in our arena, success always breeds envy. I'll manage." But Jacques's words lingered in his mind long after the kitchen had emptied for the night. All these relentless warnings kept Antoine in a constant state of anxiety.

Voiceover (Older Antoine): *"The first cracks in my confidence began to appear during those weeks. I had always believed that hard work and talent would be enough to secure my place. But the shadows gathering around me suggested otherwise."*

The next commission came not from a noble but from an ambitious merchant looking to solidify his position among the city's elite. Antoine's design for the event was a departure from his usual style: a modern, geometric pièce montée that reflected the merchant's forward-thinking sensibilities. The project was a challenge, requiring precise engineering and flawless execution. As Antoine and his team worked by twilight, a courier arrived with a package addressed to Antoine. He opened it to find a small box containing a shattered sugar sculpture—a mockery of one of his past creations. Attached is a note:

Talent is fragile. Beware whom you trust.

The message was unsigned, but its meaning was clear. Antoine's work had drawn not just admiration but malice. He clenched his fists, anger, and agitation mingling inside. Dupont found him staring at the broken shards.

"Carême," Dupont said, his tone unusually gentle. "Do not let them see your fear. Envy is a coward's weapon. Focus on your abilities. That is your strength." Antoine swallowed with an uneasiness, "Yes, Chef. Thank you."

Even with all his anxiety and fear, Antoine remained resolute, and the merchant's event was a success, the pièce montée a testament to Antoine's resilience. Guests marveled at the clean lines and bold structure, a stark contrast to the opulence of his earlier work. The merchant, pleased beyond measure, promised to spread Antoine's name among his influential associates. But as Antoine returned to Talleyrand's estate that night, he couldn't shake the feeling of being watched. The flicker of a shadow at the edge of his vision, the faint creak of footsteps behind him—they set his nerves on edge.

He quickened his pace and reached the safety of the estate's gates without incident.

Voiceover (Older Antoine): *"For all the triumphs of those days, a sense of foreboding began to creep into my life. Success had brought me into the light, but the shadows surrounding it grew darker and more menacing."*

The tensions crested one evening as Antoine prepared for a private dinner hosted by Talleyrand himself. The menu was simple but refined, intended to showcase the elegance of French cuisine. Antoine worked with such detail and care, plating each dish as if it were a work of art. As he stepped out of the kitchen to deliver the final course, a servant intercepted him. "Monsieur Carême, a message for you." Antoine took the folded paper. The note read:

Leave Paris before it's too late.

His stomach churned as he tucked the note into his pocket. He delivered the dish with a composed expression, but his mind raced. Who was behind the warnings? And how far would they go to see him undone?

That night, Antoine sought out Dupont. Dupont listened in silence as Antoine recounted the warnings and the shattered sculpture. When Antoine finished, Dupont leaned back, his expression grim. "You have a gift, Carême," Dupont said. "But gifts come with a price. The higher you climb, the more visible you become. Visibility can be as dangerous as it is rewarding."

"I will not let fear drive me from my path. This is my life, Chef. My work. I will protect it." Antoine's words are full of strength. Dupont, "Good. But be careful. Not all battles are fought in the open. Some are waged in the shadows, where the rules are different." Antoine grew increasingly cautious. He began to double-check his ingredients and tools, wary of sabotage. Jacques stayed close, offering support and an extra pair of watchful eyes. Despite the tension,

Antoine continued to push himself, determined to rise above the threats and the cowards that were behind them.

The next major commission came from an influential duchess who requested an edible replica of her sprawling summer estate. It was to be the centerpiece of an extravagant soirée, a testament to both her wealth and Carême's rising brilliance. The design was bold: marzipan columns, sugar-blown fountains, and delicate spun-sugar greenery adorning a confectionery masterpiece. Every detail had to be flawless. Antoine immersed himself in the work, barely stopping to eat or sleep. The grand kitchen, usually filled with the rhythmic clatter of kitchen staff, was empty; while the entire staff went to bed, he worked alone. The only sounds were the soft scrape of his sculpting tools and the occasional crackling of cooling sugar. He found solace in the silence until the silence was broken. A rustling. A whisper of movement behind him. He turned sharply, his pulse hammering in his ears.

Nothing.

A trick of the candlelight, perhaps. The hours of work had worn on his senses. But the unease remained, curling around him like a cold breath against his neck. He shook his head and forced himself back to work, molding the final sugar details onto the marzipan walls. But no matter how much he focused, the feeling of being watched refused to fade.

The night before the event, disaster struck. A section of the estate's sugar-glass windows shattered inexplicably; the delicate sculptures were reduced to jagged fragments on the marble counter. Antoine froze. He had handled the piece with the utmost care. There was no reason for it to break. Unless... He swallowed his unease and forced himself to work through the night, painstakingly repairing the damage, ensuring the final presentation would be nothing short of breathtaking.

When the evening arrived, the grand hall was ablaze with golden candlelight. The elite of Paris gathered, their silk gowns sweeping over polished floors as they gasped in admiration at Antoine's creation. The duchess herself was enraptured, guiding her guests through the sugar-crafted replica of her estate with the pride of an empress showing off her kingdom. Antoine stood in the shadows, exhausted yet satisfied. Another victory. Another step toward immortality in the world of culinary artistry. And yet…The feeling of unease coiled in his stomach. The warnings. The broken sculpture. The unseen movements in the night. Dupont found him before the night ended, his sharp eyes scanning the crowd before settling on Antoine. His voice was calm, but his words carried weight.

"You did well, Carême. But remember, success makes you a target. Stay vigilant." Antoine's jaw tightened. He had come too far, fought too hard to be undone by fear, and between the threatening notes, Dupont's warnings, and the sense of a lurking presence, his resolve was unshaken. He met Dupont's gaze. "I will, Chef."

Voiceover (Older Antoine):

"I learned that success was not a destination but a battlefield. Every conquest was a victory, but every victory grew the bullseye on my back. And yet, I could not turn away. The fire that drove me burned fiercely, and I wanted to see how far it could take me."

CHAPTER 9

THE PRICE OF PROMINENCE

The threats against Antoine Carême did not subside after the shattered sugar sculpture and ominous notes. If anything, they grew more insidious. Whispers followed him wherever he went, and the discomfort that had been a faint undercurrent now felt like a shadow dogging his every step. Yet Antoine did not waver. The demands of his profession consumed him, leaving little room for fear. Tensions in Talleyrand's kitchen simmered just below the surface, an unspoken battle of ambition and pride. Rivals tracked Antoine's every move, their eyes filled with a volatile mix of envy and resentment. Some whispered that he had been lucky, while others accused him of exploiting his position for personal gain. The weight of these accusations pressed heavily on Antoine, but he refused to let them distract him. His focus remained on his work and his work alone.

Voiceover (Older Antoine): *"Ambition is a double-edged sword. The same greatness that illuminates your path casts shadows in the hearts of others. I had always believed that hard work and skill would protect me, but I was beginning to understand that success brought its own dangers."*

One morning, as Antoine prepared for another high-profile banquet, Jacques burst into the kitchen. His face was pale, his usual composure replaced with alarm. "Carême," Jacques whispered urgently, pulling Antoine aside. "There's talk of sabotage. Someone plans to ruin tonight's banquet." "What do you mean? Who would do such a thing? How did you come by this information?"

Jacques shook his head. "I don't know. But be careful. They're saying it's someone within the kitchen." Jacques avoids Antoine's final question." Antoine's thoughts raced. The kitchen had always been a place of tension, but betrayal? That was a far more dangerous game. "I'll keep watch," Antoine said, his voice steady despite the knot coiling in his gut. "Thank you, Jacques."

Voiceover (Older Antoine): *"In that moment, I realized how fragile trust could be. A kitchen thrives on teamwork and being focused, but when fear, greed, and spite creep in, even the strongest bonds can fracture. I could no longer take anything—or anyone—for granted."*

The banquet's menu had been meticulously planned, featuring delicate amuse-bouches, rich entrées, and a pièce montée that pushed the boundaries of Antoine's capabilities. Inspired by the soaring arches of Gothic cathedrals, Antoine had crafted a structure of nougatine and spun sugar, its intricate spires reaching skyward. The pièce montée had to be flawless, a testament to his talent and a barrier against the whispers that threatened to undermine him.

As the preparations intensified, Antoine's vigilance sharpened. He watched his team closely, searching for any sign of sabotage. Every ingredient was inspected twice; every dish was tasted before it left the kitchen. Yet the pressure of suspicion weighed heavily on him. That evening, as Antoine worked on the finishing touches of the pièce montée, he noticed one of the younger cooks lingering near his station. The boy's hands hovered over a jar of powdered sugar, his watch darting nervously around the room. "What are you doing?" Antoine questioned, his voice cutting through the noise of the kitchen. The boy flinched, nearly dropping the jar. "N-nothing, Chef. I was just… organizing." Antoine stepped forward, his tone sharp and commanding. "Get back to your station now! The boy, with a nod, frantically and then scurried away, leaving Antoine staring at the jar. He opened it carefully and looked at its contents but found nothing unusual. Still, the encounter left him uneasy.

The banquet unfolded with all the pomp and splendor expected of Talleyrand's court. Nobles and diplomats filled the grand hall, their laughter mingling with the soft strains of a string quartet. The pièce montée was unveiled to a chorus of gasps, its golden spires glittering under the chandelier's light. Antoine watched from the shadows as the guests marveled at his creation. But the night's victory was short-lived. As the final course was served, a commotion erupted at one of the tables. A nobleman doubled over, his face pale and his breath labored. Servants rushed to his side, and panic rippled through the hall. Antoine froze, he turned toward the kitchen, where Dupont was already issuing orders to his staff. "No one leaves this room," Dupont barked. "Search everything. Find the source."

The kitchen descended into chaos as every dish, every utensil, and every ingredient was scrutinized. Antoine's breath came in shallow gasps as he reviewed his own station, his thoughts a jumble of fear and desperation. Had someone tampered with his work? Could he have missed something?

After what felt like an eternity, Dupont approached Antoine, his expression grim. "It wasn't your station," Dupont said. "The contamination came from the wine." Relief flooded Antoine, but it was short-lived. Dupont's gaze hardened. "But this will not stay confined to the truth. Rumors will spread, and they will look for someone to blame. Stay vigilant, Carême. This is far from over."

In the days that followed, the incident cast a long shadow over Talleyrand's estate. Though the nobleman recovered, the whispers of sabotage persisted. Antoine threw himself into his work in order to rise above the scandal. But the note that arrived one week later shook him to his core; this was beginning to turn fear and anxiety into immense anger:

You escaped this time. You won't be so lucky again.

Antoine crumpled the paper in his hand, his anger flaring. Whoever was behind these threats was no longer content to linger in the shadows. They were escalating, and Antoine knew he had to act. That evening, he sought out Talleyrand himself. The diplomat listened intently as Antoine recounted the events of the past weeks, Talleyrand void of emotion. "Monsieur Carême," Talleyrand said finally, "you are a valuable asset to this household. But value like success often breeds envy, as I am more than positive you are aware by now. I will have my men investigate these threats, but you must remain vigilant. Your enemies are playing a dangerous game, and so must you." Antoine's resolve hardened. "I will not let them destroy what I have built, Monseigneur." Talleyrand's mouth bent into a faint smile. "Good. Then, show them that their efforts are in vain. Let your work speak louder than their malice."

The road ahead was treacherous, but Antoine knew he could not turn back. His art form was not just his passion but his shield, weapon, and legacy. Every challenge he faced only strengthened his rise above the fray.

Voiceover (Older Antoine): *"In those days, I learned that survival within the realm of power required more than skill. It challenged resilience, cunning, and the ability to rise above the fray. The threats would not stop, but neither would I, and I vowed to forge a path that no one could extinguish."*

CHAPTER 10
A DANGEROUS ALLIANCE

The morning light streamed through the windows of Talleyrand's estate as Antoine Carême prepared for another day in the kitchen. The weight of the previous week's events stuck around, but he refused to let fear overshadow his work. His pièce montée for the evening banquet had to be impeccable as did all his work. The blueprint was a celebration of symmetry and elegance, inspired by the fountains of Versailles, with cascading layers of spun sugar and marzipan blossoms. Antoine's hands moved with preciseness as he measured sugar and flour, his focus unwavering despite the tension in the kitchen. The incident at the last banquet—and the ominous note that followed—had left its mark, but Antoine pushed the thoughts aside. There was no room for hesitation. Jacques appeared at his side, his expression grave. "Carême," Jacques began, his voice low, "there's someone here to see you. They're waiting in the storage room. They didn't say who they were but insisted it's urgent." Visitors were rare, especially ones that bypassed the estate's formal protocols. He glanced at his workbench, then sighed. "Keep an eye on the team. I'll see who it is."

Voiceover (Older Antoine): *"I had learned to be cautious by then. The threats against me had taken many forms—notes, whispers, sabotage—and each one reminded me that my position was precarious. But nothing could have prepared me for what awaited in the shadows of the storage room."*

The storage room was dimly lit, the scent of dried herbs and cured meats filling the air. A man stood in the shadows, his coat tailored but worn, his posture suggesting both authority and secrecy. Antoine's steps slowed as he approached. "Monsieur Carême," the man said, his voice smooth and measured. "I represent a party that has been interested in your... remarkable talents." Antoine's showing a mix of surprise and suspicion flickering within them. "And who might that party be?

The man stepped forward, the light catching the sharp angles of his face. "Consider us patrons of originality. We admire your work and believe your future lies beyond Talleyrand's kitchen. We can offer you opportunities that even he cannot." Antoine's jaw tightened. "I am grateful for my position here. If you wish to commission a work, you can do so through the proper channels."

The man's smile didn't waver. "This is not about a commission. It is about power, Monsieur Carême. The power that your creations can bring. Imagine a position where your artistry influences more than noble palates. Imagine shaping alliances, swaying politics, commanding the attention of kings." Antoine took a step back. "I am a chef, not a politician." "You are both," the man countered, his voice growing sharper. "Every dish you create sends a message. Every banquet is a battlefield. Talleyrand knows this, but he does not share that power. "We can." Antoine's kept his expression neutral. "And what would you ask of me in return?" The man's smile widened. "For now, only your cooperation. Consider this an invitation to a larger stage. But tread carefully, Monsieur Carême. Power is as dangerous as it is alluring." Before Antoine could respond, the man turned and disappeared into the shadows, leaving behind only the faint echo of his footsteps.

Voiceover (Older Antoine): *"That encounter was the first time I understood how deeply my work was entangled with the machinations of power. Until then, I had believed that my creations spoke only of beauty and ambition. But I began to see that they could also be weapons, wielded by those who sought to use them for their own ends."*

Antoine returned to the kitchen. Jacques stood there and gave him a questioning look, but Antoine shook his head. "Nothing to worry about," he said, though the unease in his demeanor told a different story.

The banquet that evening was once again a sensational success, a dazzling spectacle of culinary artistry and refined elegance. Gilded candelabras cast a warm, flickering glow over the long banquet table, its pristine white linen heavy with the weight of gold-rimmed porcelain and polished silver. Crystal goblets shimmered with the deep reds of vintage Bordeaux, their fragrance mingling with the intoxicating scents of roasted meats, fresh herbs, and delicately spiced sauces. The air hummed with the low murmur of aristocratic conversation, punctuated by bursts of laughter and the occasional clink of glass against glass in a toast to the evening's grandeur. At the center of it all stood Antoine's pièce montée—a towering confection of spun sugar, delicate pastillage, and sculpted nougat inspired by the symmetry and splendor of the gardens of Versailles. Elegant pavilions, minuscule fountains, and arching trellises, all rendered in sugar, recreated the majesty of the royal gardens in exquisite edible form. Gasps of admiration rippled through the room as footmen carefully wheeled it to the head of the table, each guest craning forward to admire the delicate craftsmanship. Even the most jaded of dignitaries murmured their appreciation while some discreetly examined the structure from different angles, attempting to decipher the secret of its construction.

From his seat, Talleyrand observed the scene with his usual enigmatic detachment, though Antoine caught the briefest glint of satisfaction in his host's expression. It was rare for the statesman to offer any outward sign of approval, yet there it was—a slow, deliberate nod accompanied by a glance of scrutiny. Was he, once again, assessing Antoine's worth, measuring him not only as a chef but as a man of strategic value? The thought unsettled Antoine, but he had little time to dwell on it. Even as he accepted murmured praise and appreciative glances, a shadow loomed over his thoughts. The memory of the man in the storage room clung to him like the ghost of a soured sauce—unwanted, persistent. Who was he? And, more importantly, what would his mysterious patrons demand next?

Voiceover (Older Antoine): *"Success had always been my goal, but I had not anticipated the cost. The forces around me grew more complicated and more dangerous. I realized that my artistic skills were no longer mine alone; it had become a currency in a game I did not yet understand."*

The following days brought no answers, only more questions. A package arrived at the estate, addressed to Antoine. Inside was a delicate sugar sculpture of an eagle, its wings outstretched. Beneath it lay a card with a single word:

Soon.

Antoine stared at the sculpture, it was a masterpiece, rivaling even his own work. Whoever had sent it was no amateur. They were sending a message—one he could not yet decipher. Dupont noticed the change in Antoine's demeanor. One evening, as the kitchen quieted and the fires burned low, he approached the young chef. "You've been distracted, Carême," Dupont said, his tone gruff but concerned. "What's weighing on you?"

Antoine hesitated, then turned towards Dupont. "There are forces at play that I don't understand, Chef. People who see me as more than a chef. They want something from me, but I don't know what." Dupont's eyes tightened. "Your ambitions have and will continue to draw attention, Carême. And attention draws danger. You must decide how far you're willing to go and what you're willing to risk." Antoine with a look of contemplation as Dupont's voice resonates. "Just as my sculptures stand unshaken, I will not allow anyone to tear down what I've built. But I refuse to be a mere pawn in their games." Dupont's expression unstiffened. "Good. Remember, Carême, your work is your armor. Let it speak for you, and let it protect you."

Voiceover (Older Antoine): *"In order to navigate the perilous waters ahead with caution and steadfastness. I had worked too hard to let others dictate my path. But I knew that the challenges before me were unlike anything I had faced. My journey had become a game of power, and I would have to play to win."*

The friction finally came to a head when another letter arrived and slipped under Antoine's door. This one bore no signature, only an invitation:

Meet us at the Café des Artistes at midnight. Come alone.

The invitation was a gamble, but ignoring it might be just as dangerous. He tucked the letter into his coat and sat by the window, gazing out at the darkened city.

Voiceover (Older Antoine): *"That night, I stood at a crossroads. The safe path was clear: remain in Talleyrand's service, build my legacy quietly, and avoid the tangled web of politics and power. But the other path—the one shrouded in uncertainty—promised a stage far grander than any I had imagined. The question I would ask was whether to step onto it."*

The following night, Antoine made his way to the Café des Artistes. The air was thick with tension as he entered the dimly lit establishment. A man waited at a corner table, his face obscured by the brim of his hat. Antoine approached cautiously, his every sense on high alert.

"You came," the man said, his voice familiar. It was the same figure from the storage room. Antoine sat, his posture guarded.

"I want answers. Who are you, and what do you want from me?" The man chuckled softly.

"We are facilitators of influence, Monsieur Carême. Your work has already begun to reshape how people see power and beauty. We can amplify that. But first, you must trust us." "Trust is earned,"

Antoine replied coldly. "And so far, all you've given me are riddles." The man with a slight motion as if expecting a response.

"Fair. Consider tonight the first step. Opportunities are rare, Monsieur Carême. Don't let caution keep you from seizing yours."

Antoine leaned forward. "And if I refuse?"

The man's smile faded. "Then you may find the world a colder place. Think carefully, chef. The decisions you make now will echo far into your future." The man rose, leaving a small package on the table before disappearing into the night. Antoine stared at it for a long moment before finally opening it. Inside was a sugar rose, its petals flawless, accompanied by a final note:

Every rose has thorns.

As Antoine left the Café des Artistes, the package containing the sugar rose tucked under his arm. The cryptic meeting left him unsettled, his mind a storm of unanswered questions. Who were these mysterious "facilitators," and what did they truly want from him? The streets of Paris were unusually quiet, the gas lamps casting long, flickering shadows along the cobblestones.

As he walked, his thoughts spiraled. His work had always been his refuge, a place where the chaos outside of the kitchen faded into the measurements of sugar, flour, and fire. But now, even that sanctuary felt threatened. The package he carried, with its unspoken message, was a reminder that his skill had become a currency in a game he barely understood.

Voiceover (Older Antoine): *"That night, it solidified my realization that my work had become more than art. It was a language, a weapon, a currency. The choice before me was not just about fulfilling my future—it was about survival. And as much as I wanted to walk away, I knew that the only way forward was through."*

PART III
THE PHILOSOPHER OF FOOD

CHAPTER 11
ECHOES OF INFLUENCE

The weeks following Antoine Carême's encounter with the shadowy figure at the Café des Artistes were fraught with tension. The sugar rose, left as both a gift and a warning, sat on his desk, its flawless petals a reminder of the choice he had yet to make. Though Antoine buried himself in his work, the pressure around him was mounting. Every commission felt like a test, every interaction laced with double meanings.

Tension peaked one afternoon when a summons arrived from Talleyrand. Antoine set aside the delicate sugar spire he had been shaping, his mind racing as he made his way to the diplomat's study. The room was as imposing as ever, sunlight streaming through tall windows onto shelves lined with books and maps.

"Carême," Talleyrand began without preamble, "your talents have elevated this household's reputation beyond what I could have anticipated. But success is never without its costs."

Antoine inclined his head. "I understand, Monseigneur. There have been… complications."

"Complications that you must learn to manage," Talleyrand replied, his tone measured. "I have no doubt that you've been approached by those who see your work as more than culinary. Tell me, have you given them an answer?"

Antoine hesitated. "I have not committed to anything, Monseigneur. My loyalty remains here."

A faint smile appeared on Talleyrand. "Good. But loyalty, Carême, must be guarded as fiercely as ambition. You are no longer merely a chef. Your creations are symbols, and symbols wield power. That power will attract both allies and enemies."

Antoine's pulse quickened. "What do you advise, Monseigneur?"

Talleyrand leaned back in his chair, swirling his wine. "Understand this: Alliances are as fleeting as they are essential. You must decide who you trust and who you keep at arm's length. But above all, never let anyone—friend or foe—define you. That is a lesson you must learn quickly."

Voiceover (Older Antoine): *"Talleyrand's words stayed with me long after I left his study. I had always seen myself as a true artisan devoted to perfection. But now, I began to understand that my work had become a currency rife with shifting loyalties and hidden agendas."*

Back in the kitchen, the friction between Antoine and his peers had grown palpable. While some marveled at his creations, others whispered behind his back, their envy thinly veiled. Jacques, ever the loyal friend, confronted him one evening as they scrubbed their stations.

"Carême, something's brewing," Jacques said, his voice low. "I've heard rumors that someone is planning to undermine you."

Antoine frowned with an uneasy laugh. "You always seem to be the bearer of bad news, Jacques. Do you know who?"

Jacques shook his head. "Not yet. But keep your guard up. You've made enemies, whether you intended to or not."

Antoine's jaw tightened. "I've done nothing but work myself to the bone. If that's a crime, so be it. After enduring threats, warnings, sabotage, cutthroat competition, jealousy, and the treacheries of politics, my skin has hardened to stone."

Jacques sighed. "Talent and hard work don't just earn respect; they make you a target."

Antoine scoffed. "That's a familiar tune, something I hear all too often."

The turning point came during preparations for a banquet for another visiting ambassador. Antoine's centerpiece was among his most ambitious yet: a sugar sculpture depicting a dove mid-flight, surrounded by cascading ribbons of caramel and marzipan olive branches. The theme of peace was fitting, given the political tensions swirling around Napoleon's court.

As the banquet drew nearer, Antoine noticed small but unsettling signs of tampering or, worse, sabotage. A mold he needed for the sculpture went missing, only to reappear in a different part of the kitchen. A batch of caramel burned inexplicably while he was momentarily distracted. Each incident was minor on its own, but together, they painted a troubling picture.

To protect his work, Antoine began arriving earlier and staying later than anyone else. He tasted every ingredient, ensuring they were not contaminated, tested every tool, and kept a close eye on his station. But the atmosphere in the kitchen remained charged, and Antoine's growing paranoia began to wear on him.

Voiceover (Older Antoine): *"The sabotage was subtle but deliberate. It was not enough to ruin me outright, but enough to keep me on edge, to make me doubt my own instincts, where precision was everything, doubt was a dangerous enemy."*

The night of the banquet arrived, Antoine's pièce montée stood proudly in the center of the grand dining hall— The sugar sculpture depicting a dove mid-flight, magnificent columns surrounded by ribbons of caramel and marzipan olive branches. Gilded candelabras bathed the confection in a warm glow, making the spun sugar filigree shimmer like frost on a winter morning. Guests murmured their admiration as they entered, drawn first to the spectacle, then to their seats, anticipation thick in the air.

The feast began without a hitch, course after course emerging from the kitchen with seamless precision. But a sharp gasp echoed through the hall just as the final entrée was cleared. A noblewoman stood with her silk glove pressed against her mouth; her expression twisted in shock.

Then, the whispers started.

"The sculpture…" someone muttered.

Antoine turned, his stomach twisting at the sight. His pièce montée—his magnum opus—was crumbling before his eyes. The once-majestic structure, built with days of labor and precision, had begun to sag. The sugar columns supporting the central archway cracked, sending a shower of delicate shards onto the table below. A wing from the sugar dove broke off, landing in a fine dusting of caramelized ruins.

Gasps filled the room.

Antoine rushed forward, heart hammering. This wasn't a mistake—he had reinforced every joint and tested every support. Someone had done this.

Dupont, ever watchful, stepped to his side, his expression dark. "This was no accident."

Antoine's mind raced. Who would dare sabotage his work? He turned to the kitchen doors, suddenly aware of every lingering glance, every hushed conversation over the past few days. He had competitors—rivals who would see him fall. And beyond that, he had caught whispers of political tensions simmering beneath the surface of these gatherings.

"This was meant to humiliate me," Antoine murmured, his hands clenching into fists.

Dupont's voice was low, measured. "More than that, Carême. It was meant to make you doubt yourself."

A slow breath left Antoine's lips, but his resolve only hardened. Whoever had done this underestimated him.

Voiceover (Older Antoine): *"That night, I learned that sabotage wasn't always a direct attack—it could be quiet, insidious, striking where it hurt most. It was never just about food. It was about power. And in the world I had stepped into, there was no room for weakness."*

CHAPTER 12
AN UNEXPECTED ENCOUNTER

The night air was cool, and the faint strains of a melody pulled him from his reverie. It was a soft, haunting tune played on a violin, drifting from the direction of a small park. Drawn by the music, Antoine found himself wandering toward the source, his steps slowing as the sound grew clearer.

Under a grove of trees, a young woman stood, her bow gliding effortlessly across the strings of her instrument. Her posture was graceful, her eyes closed as though lost in the emotion of the music. The melody spoke of longing and hope, each note resonating deeply within him. Antoine hesitated, not wanting to interrupt, but the music stirred something he hadn't felt in weeks: calm.

When the piece ended, the woman opened her eyes she smiled softly. "You look like a man with much on his mind."

Antoine stepped closer, offering a polite nod. "And you play like someone who understands such burdens."

Her smile widened. "Music often carries what words cannot." She lowered her violin and extended a hand. "Hélène. And you?"

"Antoine Carême," he replied, shaking her hand. "It's a pleasure to meet you."

Hélène tilted her head, studying him. "Carême... the chef? I've heard of you. Your creations are said to be as much art as they are food."

Antoine chuckled, the tension easing. "And your playing is as much soul as it is music. What brings you out here at this hour?"

"The same thing that brought you," she said. "A need for clarity. The city can feel so heavy sometimes. Out here, it's easier to think."

Antoine understands all too well. "Clarity is a rare thing these days."

"For you, perhaps," Hélène said, her tone curious. "What troubles you, Monsieur Carême?"

Antoine hesitated the weight of his recent encounters pressing down on him. But something about Hélène's calm presence invited honesty. "I've found myself at a crossroads. My work has brought me opportunities I never imagined, but they come with complications I'm unsure how to navigate."

Hélène studied him thoughtfully, her expression kind but penetrating. "Great talent often draws both admiration and envy. But you must decide what you value most. Is it the work itself or the influence it brings?"

Antoine considered what she said. "I used to think it was the work. But now I wonder if the two can even be separated."

Hélène's with a softer tone, "Perhaps they can't. But you should never lose sight of why you began. Ambition is a fine thing, but it should never outpace your passion."

For a moment, the noise in Antoine's mind quieted. "You're wiser than your years suggest, Mademoiselle."

Hélène laughed, the sound light and melodic. "Wisdom comes from observation, not age. And Paris is a city full of lessons if you know where to look."

Antoine smiled, feeling a sense of connection he hadn't expected. "And what lessons has Paris taught you?"

"That beauty and chaos often walk hand in hand," she said, glancing toward the distant glow of the city. "And that sometimes, the most important thing is remembering why you started in the first place."

Settling into Antoine's mind like seeds waiting to take root were her words. Before he could respond, the church bell tolled midnight, its deep chime echoing across the city. Hélène glanced toward the sound and sighed. "It seems my time here is up. I must go."

"Will I see you again?" Antoine asked, surprising himself with the question.

Hélène paused, her smile returning. "Paris is small for those who seek its heart. I'm certain our paths will cross again." With that, she turned and disappeared into the shadows, leaving Antoine alone under the trees.

Voiceover (Older Antoine):

"Meeting Hélène was like encountering a quiet breeze amid a storm. She didn't solve my problems but reminded me of something I had nearly forgotten: the reason I began. In her presence, my work seemed less burdensome and passion more vivid. I didn't know it then, but she would become a thread woven deeply into the fabric of my life."

As Antoine made his way back to Talleyrand's estate, her words echoed in his mind. The weight of his recent struggles hadn't disappeared, but it felt lighter, as though someone had helped him shoulder the burden.

Entering his quarters, Antoine moved with a slow, deliberate motion, his gaze fixed ahead, lost in thought. Without breaking from his trance-like state, he pulled out his desk chair and lowered himself into it, the weight of his reflections settling heavily upon him. He pulled out one of his old sketches, a design for a pièce montée he had created years ago before his name carried weight. The lines were simple but full of wonder, unburdened by the pressures of reputation or influence.

He traced the drawing with his finger, Hélène's voice replaying in his mind: **"Remember why you started."**

Antoine immediately pulled out a fresh sheet of parchment. He hesitated for only a moment before setting his pencil to the page, his strokes guided by something beyond mere technique. The design unfolding before him was unlike anything he had crafted in recent years, a return to the purity of his earliest inspirations yet layered with the sophistication and mastery he had since acquired. It was a fusion of past and future, innocence and experience, longing and purpose.

As the night deepened, his hand moved with fluid precision, tracing the vision that had taken root in his mind. This piece would be different—less an ostentatious display of skill and more a reflection of something intimate, something profound. It would not simply impress; it would resonate.

By the time the first light of dawn crept through the window, Antoine set down his pencil and exhaled. Before him was the completed design—a breathtaking sculpture inspired by the natural elegance of a weeping willow, its sugar branches sweeping gracefully downward, adorned with delicate blossoms of rose-petal-thin pastillage. Beneath the canopy, tiers of spun sugar formed the illusion of cascading waterfalls, their filigree strands catching the light like silk threads. Caramelized ribbons intertwined through the structure like golden vines, winding up toward the apex, where a single, translucent sugar bird perched as if caught mid-song.

It was a piece that spoke of movement and stillness, fragility and strength. Growth. Transformation. A celebration of everything he had been and everything he was becoming.

Voiceover (Older Antoine):

"Hélène's words stayed with me long after that night. She reminded me that my life—my art—would be hollow without passion. True mastery was not in dazzling the eyes alone but in stirring the soul. It was a lesson I would carry with me, even as the path ahead darkened."

With renewed purpose, Antoine threw himself into his work. The tensions and silent threats that lingered in the background had not vanished, but he no longer allowed them to dictate his craft. He worked deep into the nights, refining his creation with the care of a composer fine-tuning a melody.

When the sculpture was unveiled at the next banquet, the response was unlike anything he had experienced before. The guests did not simply admire it—they were moved by it. Conversations hushed, replaced by an awed silence as they took in the elegant structure, the softness in its details, the quiet poetry in its form.

Talleyrand himself approached, his keen gaze lingering on the sculpture before shifting to Antoine.

"Extraordinary, Carême," he murmured, his voice tinged with something rarely heard reflection. "This is more than beautiful. It is profound. You've reminded us all of something we didn't realize we had forgotten."

Antoine bowed his head. "Thank you, Monseigneur. That means more than you know."

As the evening wore on and admiration continued to flow, Antoine's thoughts drifted to Hélène. There had been something in her music—a depth, a clarity—that he had only now captured in sugar. He did not know when or how, but he felt certain their paths would cross again.

CHAPTER 13
A TARGET IN SUGAR
AND STONE

Antoine Carême returned to Talleyrand's estate feeling renewed after his encounter with Hélène, yet the quiet wisdom she imparted couldn't shelter him from the mounting pressures of his reality. His growing reputation had become both a blessing and a curse, and the intrigue surrounding his life only deepened. Antoine noticed subtle changes around the estate. The kitchen, once alive with camaraderie, now felt tense. Whispers and sidelong glances seemed to follow him, their source unclear. It was as though an invisible thread of suspicion wove itself through his every move. He tried to focus, pouring his energy into a towering pièce montée for an upcoming banquet.

One afternoon, Dupont summoned Antoine to the kitchen's storage room. His face was lined with worry, his usual gruff demeanor replaced with something closer to concern.

"Carême," Dupont began, his voice low, "there's been a rumor—a dangerous one. Some say you're working with outside forces, undermining Talleyrand's interests."

Antoine's tensed up. "That's not true, Chef. My loyalty is here."

Dupont studied him carefully, searching Antoine's face for any hint of deception. "Rumors don't need truth to cause damage. Someone is stirring the pot, and their aim is clear: to see you fall. Be vigilant, Carême. Whoever started this isn't trying to expose you—they're trying to destroy you. This kitchen thrives on the team and trust. Lose one, and everything collapses."

Careme's mind was in a flurry. "I understand. Thank you, Chef."

Dupont placed a heavy hand on his shoulder. "Don't give them a reason to doubt you, Carême. And watch your back."

Voiceover (Older Antoine):

"Dupont's warning struck deeper than I let on. I had been so focused on perfection that I failed to see how shifts around me. My ambition had painted a target on my back, and I was unprepared for the arrows that followed."

The tension in the kitchen was palpable in the following days. The team worked in near silence, their usual camaraderie replaced by wary glances and hushed conversations. Antoine noticed Jacques growing more distant, his easy smiles replaced by furtive looks. Even his trusted friend seemed hesitant to speak, as though proximity to Antoine might bring trouble.

One evening, as Antoine prepared the components for a new pièce montée, Jacques stood near where he was working. Looking directly at Antoine and hesitating before speaking.

"Carême," Jacques said, his tone uncertain. "There's something I need to tell you."

Antoine set down his tools, his brow furrowing. "What is it?"

Jacques glanced around, ensuring they were alone. "I overheard something—a group of nobles at the last banquet. They were speaking about you. They think you're… aligning with the wrong people."

"And what do you think?"

Jacques hesitated, then sighed. "I think you're walking a fine line. I believe in you, but not everyone does. Be careful, Antoine. People are watching."

Antoine's chest was constricting, but he forced himself to nod. "Thank you, Jacques. I'll be careful."

Jacques didn't respond and walked away, leaving Antoine alone with his thoughts.

Voiceover (Older Antoine):

"Jacques's words stayed with me long after that night. Trust, once abundant, now felt scarce. I began to see the shadows lurking behind every corner, the faces in the crowd I could no longer read. The world I had once navigated so confidently was everchanging beneath my feet."

That week's banquet was among the most extravagant, each gathering surpassing the last in grandeur and complexity—mirroring the rise of his reputation and the ever-growing demands placed upon him. Every dish was a masterpiece, every detail painstakingly planned. The pièce montée was a towering creation inspired by Paris's bridges, its arches made of nougatine, and its tiers adorned with delicate sugar flowers. It was one of Antoine's most ambitious works to date, a testament to both his technical skill and his creative vision.

As the dessert was unveiled, a hushed murmur of awe spread through the hall like a wave. Antoine stood at the edge of the room, closely surveying as guests marveled at his creation. His expression mirrored the one he had worn years ago, the very first time his work had earned admiration. Across the room, Talleyrand approached the centerpiece, his gaze lingering on the intricate details, his expression unreadable.

"It is extraordinary," Talleyrand said, his voice low but clear. "You have outdone yourself, Carême."

"Thank you, Monseigneur."

But before the moment could linger, a loud crash shattered the air. The room turned toward the sound to see one of the dessert carts overturned; its contents spilled across the floor. Gasps filled the room as a servant scrambled to clean the mess, their face pale with panic.

Antoine's stomach twisted as he noticed a figure retreating into the shadows near the kitchen doors. Someone had orchestrated this.

Dupont appeared at Antoine's side, his face thunderous. "Find out who's responsible," he hissed. "And fix this. Now."

"Right away, chef," as immediately moved to restore order. He directed the staff with calmness and care, ensuring the banquet continued without further incident. The pièce montée remained untouched, its elegance undiminished, but the damage to the evening's atmosphere was undeniable. Whispers of sabotage swirled among the guests, and Antoine felt the weight of their scrutiny.

Voiceover (Older Antoine):

"That night was a turning point. The crash of the dessert cart was not just an accident—it was a declaration. Someone wanted to see me fall, and they were willing to tear apart my reputation to do it. But I refused to let them succeed. My work had always been my shield, and I vowed to make it impenetrable."

As the estate quieted and the guests departed, Antoine found himself alone in the kitchen, the shattered remnants of the evening's desserts scattered across the counters. He began to clean, his movements slow and deliberate. He didn't notice Dupont enter until he spoke. "You did well tonight, considering the circumstances," Dupont said crustily. "But this isn't over." Antoine straightened, his jaw tight. "I know." Dupont with an expression of seriousness. "Good. Because the people coming after you—they don't care about your talent. They care about what you represent. Make sure you're worth the fight." Antoine, with a hardened expression. "I will."

As Dupont left, Antoine stood in the quiet kitchen, his fists clenched. The path was hazardous, but he would not falter. He had built his reputation on precision and the love he had for his art, and he would defend it with everything he had.

Voiceover (Older Antoine):

"The pressures of that night solidified something within me—a realization that I had to protect what I had built and a knowing that I could. The sabotage was not a warning anymore; it was a declaration of war, and I had never been one to back down from a challenge or fight. If they wanted to test me, I would show them that my work was unbreakable no matter what they threw at me."

CHAPTER 14
THREADS OF DECEPTION

The days following the disastrous banquet passed in tense silence. Antoine Carême's life had become a delicate balancing act—repairing his damaged reputation while untangling the web of forces working against him. Though the whispers of sabotage refused to die, Antoine found himself increasingly focused on uncovering the source. Every glance in the kitchen seemed laced with suspicion, and camaraderie among the staff felt strained, as though trust had been fractured beyond repair.

One evening, as Antoine reviewed designs for his next masterpiece, a knock echoed through his quarters. The sound startled him; few dared interrupt his private moments, especially in recent weeks. Opening the door, Antoine found Jacques standing there, his expression a mix of guilt and urgency.

"Antoine," Jacques began, stepping inside before the chef could invite him. "We need to talk. Now."

Antoine closed the door behind him and gestured toward a chair. "What is it?"

Jacques hesitated, running a hand through his hair, his usual composure replaced with an edge of nervous energy. "I've been trying to protect you, but things have gotten out of control. There's someone in the kitchen working against you, and I think they're planning something worse."

Antoine couldn't help but wonder—why was it always Jacques bringing the warnings and news? Why only him, never anyone else? A flicker of doubt crept in. Was Jacques involved somehow? Playing both sides? He had trusted him once, but now, under these strained circumstances, that trust felt fragile, slipping through his fingers before he could hold onto it.

Jacques sat, avoiding Antoine's hard-bitten look. "I didn't want to accuse anyone without proof. But after what happened at the banquet... I think it's Julien."

Antoine frowned. Julien was a quiet, capable apprentice who rarely drew attention. "Julien? He's never shown any sign of animosity."

Jacques shook his head. "That's the point. He's been careful—too careful. Last week, I caught him near your workstation. When I confronted him, he claimed he was checking supplies. I didn't think much of it then, but now..."

Antoine leaned back, his thoughts racing. "If Julien is involved, we need to act before he does more damage. But we need proof."

Voiceover (Older Antoine): *"The world I belonged to; the greatest threats are often the ones you least expect. Trust, once shaken, is a fragile thing, and suspicion can rot even the strongest foundations."*

The next morning, Antoine arrived in the kitchen before dawn, feeling the weight of Jacques's warning. He watched as the staff filtered in; he displayed a sort of trance-like gaze, carefully observing Julien's movements. The apprentice seemed unremarkable, methodically preparing his station as always. But something about his deliberate precision now seemed calculated, almost too perfect.

As the day progressed, Antoine lingered near Julien, feigning casual oversight while noting every action. When Julien left his station briefly, Antoine seized the opportunity to inspect his workspace. Beneath a pile of folded towels, he found a small vial of an unmarked substance. He pocketed the vial and returned to his station, his thoughts swirling with questions. Who had given Julien this? And why?

That evening, Antoine approached Dupont in his office, laying the vial on the desk. Dupont's expression darkened as he picked it up, turning it over in his hand.

"What is this?" Dupont asked, his voice low.

"I found it at Julien's station," Antoine replied. "I don't know what it is, but I don't believe it belongs in our kitchen."

Dupont leaned back in his chair, "This could ruin us if word gets out. Leave this with me. I'll handle it."

Antoine hesitated. "Shouldn't we confront Julien directly?"

Dupont shook his head. "Not yet. If we're wrong, we'll destroy an innocent man's career. If we're right... we need to understand the full scope of what we're dealing with."

The next few days passed in a haze of tension. Dupont's investigation was discreet, but Antoine felt the weight of it in every interaction. Julien's behavior remained unchanged, his movements calm and deliberate, as if he knew he was being watched. The atmosphere in the kitchen was suffocating, the staff's usual chatter replaced by an uneasy silence. Even Jacques seemed more withdrawn, offering only brief updates when prompted.

The breakthrough came late one evening. Dupont summoned Antoine to the storage room, his expression grim. "I had the vial tested," Dupont said without preamble. "It's a bittering agent. Harmless in small amounts, but enough to ruin a dish—and a reputation." Antoine's stomach turned. "Then Julien—" Dupont nodded. "He's been tampering with your work. I found traces of the substance in a dish from the banquet." Antoine clenched his fists. "We need to confront him before this happens again." "We will," Dupont said, his voice steady. "But this isn't just about Julien. Someone put him up to this. Julien is not the type that acts alone."

The confrontation was swift. Julien was summoned to Dupont's office, where the vial was laid before him. His face paled, his composure cracking under the weight of their questions. At first, he denied everything, but the truth began to spill under Dupont's relentless scrutiny. "It wasn't my idea," Julien stammered, his hands trembling. "I was approached by someone—a noble. He said if I caused a small failure, it would weaken Carême's standing and earn me a favor." "Who?" Antoine demanded, his voice intense and sharp. Julien hesitated, "I don't know his name. He wore a mask. But he said it would benefit us both." Dupont leaned forward, his expression fierce. "And you believed him? You risked this entire kitchen for a faceless promise?" Julien hung his head, silent.

Voiceover (Older Antoine): *"Julien's betrayal was a bitter pill to swallow. He wasn't a rival or a stranger—he was one of us. Yet his actions revealed a deeper truth: the forces against me were not limited to the kitchen; they also reached into the halls of power, where envy brewed dangerous alliances."*

Julien was cast out from Talleyrand's service the next morning, his departure like a severed limb, leaving a silent, unsettling void in the kitchen. But Antoine knew this was no simple dismissal. The precision of it all gnawed at him—Julien wasn't the mastermind, merely a piece sacrificed in a game far greater than he had realized. Someone with reach, with power, had orchestrated this from the shadows. And they were still out there. Watching. Waiting. The timing and execution were too perfect. How did they know exactly who to target? Who to manipulate? And, more chillingly, how close could they get to him without ever revealing themselves? That evening, Antoine found himself alone in the kitchen, the dim light casting long shadows across the counters. As he cleaned his station, Dupont appeared, his presence heavy with unspoken thoughts. Were they also involved in the previous attempts at sabotage?

"You were right to bring this to me," Dupont said, his voice edged with steel. "But don't fool yourself—this is far from over." "I know," Antoine replied, his gaze unwavering. "And when it comes, I'll be ready."

Dupont's usually tough expression lessened. "Good. Because the people coming after you—they don't care about your talent. They care about what you represent. Make sure you're worth the fight."

As Dupont left, Antoine stood in the quiet kitchen, his mind churning. The battle taking place was no longer just about perfection or reputation—it was about survival. And Antoine was determined to emerge victorious.

Voiceover (Older Antoine): *"The road ahead was more precarious than I had imagined. But I knew one thing with certainty: my work was my shield, weapon, and voice. And I would wield it with precision and purpose, no matter the cost."*

PART IV
A LEGACY DEFINED

CHAPTER 15
ALLIES AND ENEMIES

The dismissal of Julien from Talleyrand's kitchen brought a brief but fragile sense of relief to Antoine Carême. Yet, the revelation that his enemies extended beyond the estate's walls left him grappling with a new, unsettling reality. Whispers of intrigue and betrayal continued to swirl, making it clear that Julien had been nothing more than a pawn in a larger, more sinister game. Antoine threw himself into his work, his innovations were becoming increasingly intricate and ambitious. Yet, the very perfection of his creations seemed to heighten the tension around him. Colleagues who once praised him now watched him with wary eyes, their expressions unreadable. The kitchen, once a sanctuary, had become a battlefield.

Voiceover (Older Antoine): *"The dismissal of Julien was not the end of the struggle; it was only the beginning. Trust had been shaken, and suspicion hung in the air like smoke. My success had drawn admiration, but it had also drawn enemies, both seen and unseen. In those days, I learned that resilience was not enough—strategy was just as vital."*

One evening, as the last light of day faded, Antoine was in the estate's library. The ornate room, with its towering shelves and flickering candlelight, offered a rare reprieve from the tension that filled his days. He poured over a book on classical architecture, seeking inspiration for his next pièce. The intricate columns and vaulted ceilings sketched on the pages offered solace in their symmetry, a stark contrast to the chaos around him.

The soft creak of the library door broke the silence. Antoine glanced up to see Hélène entering, her presence a beacon of calm in the storm.

"Still working?" Hélène's voice was warm, cutting through the tension that had settled over Antoine.

Antoine offered a faint smile. "Always. What brings you here?"

Hélène stepped closer, her curious stare settling on the book in his hands. "I wanted to thank you for the dessert at the last banquet. It was breathtaking. But it seems I'm not the only one who noticed. I've heard there's been trouble."

Antoine's smile faltered. "You hear quickly."

Hélène tilted her head. "Paris reveals its smallness to those who pay attention. I reserve my attention for those who create beauty in a world that neglects it."

Antoine sighed, setting the book aside. "It seems my work has drawn more than admiration. Envy, ambition… sabotage."

Hélène frowned, pulling a chair beside him. "Sabotage? Do you know who's behind it?"

"Not entirely," Antoine admitted. "Julien was the instrument, but not the hand. Someone powerful is trying to tear me down."

She placed a hand on his arm, her touch grounding him. "Antoine, you've built something extraordinary. That frightens people who see only their own limitations. But you don't have to face this alone." As they sat together in the quiet library, it had been weeks since Antoine felt something good inside; he instantly felt the weight on his shoulders lift, if only for a moment.

Voiceover (Older Antoine): *"Meeting Hélène had been a quiet revolution in my life. Her insight and calm were a salve to the chaos, and her presence became a reminder of why I had started this journey in the first place. She was more than an ally; she was an anchor."*

The next morning, Dupont approached Antoine with unexpected news. "Talleyrand has received a request for you to prepare a banquet at the home of the Duke of Orléans," Dupont said. "This is no ordinary commission. The duke is a man of influence, wealth, and power, and all of Paris will be at this event."

Antoine straightened. "Do you think this is connected to the sabotage?"

Dupont's expression was unreadable. "I don't know. But I do know that you can't afford another misstep. The duke's household is not as controlled as ours. Be vigilant."

"I'll prepare for every possibility, chef."

The Duke of Orléans, Louis-Philippe, was a complex figure in French society. Known for his liberal leanings and cultivated image as a patron of the arts, he often straddled the line between aristocracy and the rising bourgeoisie. Hosting a banquet for the duke was not merely a culinary endeavor; it was a performance on one of the grandest stages in Paris.

The duke's kitchen was grand but chaotic. Servants scurried under the direction of a head chef whose authority seemed more bark than bite. Antoine quickly established order, his quiet confidence commanding respect. His pièce montée for the evening was a bold departure: a reinterpretation of a Grecian temple with fluted columns of nougatine and a domed roof of spun sugar. Each detail was shaped to reflect strength and elegance—a subtle message of resilience in the face of adversity.

As the evening unfolded, Antoine couldn't ignore the feeling of being watched. A shadow seemed to follow him, always at the edge of his vision. Twice, he caught servants whispering and glancing in his direction, their expressions unreadable. When the pièce montée was unveiled in the grand dining hall, the reaction was immediate and overwhelming. Gasps of admiration filled the room, and the duke himself rose to once over the creation more closely.

"Ingenious," the duke declared, his voice carrying across the hall. "Monsieur Carême, you have outdone yourself."

"Thank you, Your Grace."

As the applause subsided, Antoine caught sight of a man lingering near the hall entrance, his face obscured by the contrasting lighting. The man's posture was stiff, looking directly at Antoine. Before he could investigate further, the figure slipped away.

Voiceover (Older Antoine): *"The Duke's banquet was a defining moment in my career, but greatness rarely comes without consequence. The shadowed figure lingering at the edge of the hall would remain in my thoughts for days, a silent warning that success always demands a price.*

"Returning to Talleyrand's estate, Antoine found a letter waiting for him. The seal was unfamiliar, but the message was a vague warning like the others:"

Beware the company you keep. Even the brightest stars can be extinguished.

Antoine crumpled the letter. The relentless war for his place in the culinary realm had become a battle for his continued existence. But he would not be deterred. This was more than a calling; it was his weapon, and he would wield it with relentless resolve.

Voiceover (Older Antoine): *"Enemies closed in from all sides, blind to the depths of my resolve. My work had always been my sanctuary, but now it became the force that would undo those who sought to bring me down. The world dared to test me, and I was ready to show that I would not fall."*

CHAPTER 16
A FATEFUL INVITATION

The following days at Talleyrand's estate were tumultuous. For Antoine Carême, life had become a delicate balance. Each commission brought new challenges and opportunities, but they also sharpened the scrutiny he faced. Success had become a currency he could not afford to lose; failure was a shadow he refused to let take shape. It was during one such busy afternoon in the kitchen, as Antoine reviewed sketches for an elaborate pièce montée inspired by Versailles, that Dupont approached him, his expression as unreadable as ever.

"Monsieur Carême," Dupont said, handing him a sealed envelope. "This just arrived from His Excellency."

Antoine took the envelope, noting the Talleyrand crest stamped in crimson wax. He broke the seal carefully, his pulse quickening as he read the contents:

Monsieur Carême,

You are hereby invited to attend a private gathering at the residence of the Marquise de Lavoisier. This event will bring together some of France's most esteemed figures. Your presence is requested not merely as a chef but as a guest. I trust you will represent this household with the same excellence that defines your work.

Antoine reread the letter. A guest? He had attended countless events but always as a creator, never as an equal among the elite. This was uncharted territory.

"You've earned this," Dupont said, his voice softer than usual. "But tread carefully. These gatherings are not just social; they're mazes of power, politics, and battlegrounds. And not everyone there will see your presence as welcome."

Antoine folded the letter with deliberate precision. "Thank you, Chef. I'll prepare for whatever may come."

Voiceover (Older Antoine):

"That invitation was more than a summons—it was a test. To stand as an equal among the elite was a dream I had scarcely allowed myself to imagine. Yet I knew that beneath the glittering surface of Parisian society lay currents as treacherous as any storm."

The evening of the gathering arrived swiftly. Antoine stood outside the grand residence of the Marquise de Lavoisier, his coat freshly tailored and his hair neatly combed. The building was a masterpiece of neoclassical design, its columns and intricate carvings illuminated by flickering gas lamps. He drew a steadying breath and stepped inside. The interior was breathtaking. Chandeliers sparkled overhead, casting a warm glow over the polished marble floors. The air buzzed with conversation, a symphony of laughter and whispers mingling with the faint strains of a string quartet. Nobles, diplomats, and luminaries of Parisian society filled the room, their attire as opulent as their surroundings. Antoine felt their gazes as he entered—some curious, others appraising. His posture was more erect, reminding himself why he was there. He was not merely a chef; he was a creator whose work had captured the imagination of Paris. Antoine, unable to seek solace in his kitchen, was unthinkable, yet he found himself thrust onto an entirely new stage. The unfamiliarity of it all held an unsettling weight.

"Ah, Monsieur Carême," a voice called. Turning, he found the Marquise de Lavoisier approaching. She was a striking woman, her presence commanding yet elegant. She extended a gloved hand, which Antoine took with a slight bow.

"Marquise," he said, his voice steady. "What an honor; thank you for the invitation."

Her lips formed a faint smile. "You have become the talk of Paris, Monsieur. It seemed only fitting to introduce you to those who shape its destiny." Antoine's keeping his composure. "I'm honored to be here."

Voiceover (Older Antoine):

"Stepping into that room was like walking onto a stage I hadn't known existed. Every glance, every word carried weight, and I realized that my creations had brought me not just acclaim but rather a place in an ocean governed by power and perception."

As the evening unfolded, Antoine navigated the room with careful grace. He answered questions about his work with self-effacement, deflecting the more probing inquiries with practiced ease. It wasn't long before he encountered a familiar face.

"Monsieur Carême," Hélène's voice was a welcome reprieve. She approached with a glass of champagne in hand, her smile warm and knowing. "Hélène," Antoine said, a genuine smile breaking through his carefully measured demeanor. "I didn't expect to see you here." "And I didn't expect you to step into this world so effortlessly," she replied, her tone teasing but kind. "How are you finding it?"

Antoine chuckled softly. "It feels like walking a tightrope. One misstep, and…" He gestured vaguely, letting the implication hang in the air.

Hélène's expression relaxed. "You're doing better than most. Come, let's step outside for a moment. The garden is quieter." Grateful for the reprieve, Antoine followed her into the cool night air. The garden was a serene contrast to the opulence inside, its pathways lit by lanterns and lined with fragrant blooms.

"There are those inside who see you as a threat," Hélène said quietly as they walked. "Not because of anything you've done, but because of what you represent. You've risen on merit, Antoine. As you are well ware that with most, that's unsettling."

Antoine's expression darkened. "I've earned everything through hard work; why should that make me a threat? Honestly, Hélène, nothing shocks me anymore. I've learned to anticipate the unexpected and navigate the complexities of the world I belong to."

"Antoine, to answer your question, it reminds them that their power is not absolute," Hélène said simply. "Be careful, Antoine. Trust is a luxury you cannot afford." They returned to the party and a warning etched into his mind like a faint but persistent melody.

Voiceover (Older Antoine):

"Hélène had a way of seeing through the masks people wore, and she had no patience for the illusions they clung to. Her insight was a gift, but also a reminder of the fragility of the surroundings I was navigating."

As the evening progressed, the guests began to disperse; Antoine found himself alone near the grand staircase. A man approached, his face partially obscured by the brim of his hat.

"Monsieur Carême," the man said, his voice low and measured. "A word of advice: success is a dangerous game. The higher you climb, the more you must guard your footing."

Antoine tensed, "And who might you be to offer such advice?"

The man smiled faintly. "A friend, if you're wise. An enemy if you're careless. Choose your allies carefully, chef. Not all of them will hold your best interests at heart." Before Antoine could respond, the man disappeared into the crowd, leaving him with more questions than answers.

Voiceover (Older Antoine):

"That night, I caught a glimpse of the full scope of the forces at play. I was no longer just a chef or an artist. I was a player in a game far larger than I had ever imagined—a game where my abilities were both my greatest weapon and vulnerability."

Returning to Talleyrand's estate, Antoine found another letter waiting for him. The seal was unfamiliar, but the message was clear:

Be mindful of those around you; trust can be a dangerous illusion. Even the brightest flames can be snuffed out in the dark.

Voiceover (Older Antoine):

"The gathering at the Marquise's estate was more than a milestone; it was a revelation. Not just for my career but for understanding the treacherous world I had entered. The path ahead grew more dangerous, yet turning back was never a consideration. The deception, the threats, the warnings, the sabotage, each battle had sharpened my mind and fortified my resolve. My enemies had unknowingly forged something they never anticipated."

CHAPTER 17
AN OFFER FROM THE EAST

The days following the Marquise's gathering were hectic, yet Antoine's thoughts rarely strayed from the cryptic warnings and shadowy figures encircling his life. His culinary achievements had catapulted him to new heights, but with fame came an inevitable price. It was in this charged atmosphere that a courier arrived one frost-laden morning bearing an envelope with the double-headed eagle of the Russian Imperial Court.

Dupont handed the letter to Antoine with a knowing look. "It seems your abilities are not just admired in Paris. The Tsar himself seeks your touch." Antoine took the envelope, the weight of its significance pressing against his palm. Breaking the wax seal, he unfolded the thick parchment. The script was delicate, its strokes deliberate:

Monsieur Carême,

His Imperial Majesty, Tsar Alexander I of Russia, has heard of your extraordinary talents and wishes to extend an invitation. You are requested to journey to St. Petersburg to oversee the creation of a banquet celebrating the conclusion of a significant treaty. Your artistry is highly regarded, and your presence is most desired.
– Mikhail Vorontsov, Imperial Court Steward

St. Petersburg—Russia's gilded capital, where palaces glistened under layers of frost and intrigue wove through every corridor. It was an unparalleled opportunity, but it also carried immense risk.

Dupont studied Antoine's expression. "It's an honor, yes, but Russia is no Paris. Its court is steeped in opulence and secrecy, and the Tsar... well, Alexander is not a man easily understood. You'll need more than skill to navigate."

Antoine folded the letter carefully, his voice steady. "The stakes are high, but so is the reward. This isn't just an invitation—it's a test."

Voiceover (Older Antoine):

"The invitation to St. Petersburg marked a defining moment in my life. In Paris, it was to shape the taste of a city but to serve the Russian court meant presenting on a much larger stage. It was both an honor and a challenge, one that exacted every ounce of courage and creativity I possessed."

St. Petersburg and the Tsar's Mystique

The journey to St. Petersburg was arduous, stretching across icy plains and through dense forests blanketed in snow. Each night, Antoine sketched tirelessly by the dimness of the candles, his hands tracing the lines of a grand pièce montée that would embody the majesty of the Russian Empire. When he finally arrived, the Winter Palace rose before him like a vision from a fairy tale, its golden domes gleaming under the pale winter sun. Inside, the opulence was almost overwhelming. Chandeliers cascaded light across marble floors, walls were adorned with gilded frames and imperial insignias, and courtiers in lavish furs and silks moved with practiced grace. Their conversations were hushed but pointed as they sized up the French chef who had captured their Tsar's attention.

Mikhail Vorontsov, the Imperial Court Steward, greeted Antoine with a measured nod. He was tall and composed, his every movement calculated. "Monsieur Carême, the Tsar is eager to see your work. This banquet is no ordinary celebration—it is a demonstration of Russia's unity and power. Failure is not an option."

Antoine inclined his head. "I will not disappoint."

Vorontsov regarded him for a moment before his voice dropped to a low murmur. "Tread carefully, Monsieur. St. Petersburg is built on grand façades, but beneath them lies a tangle of intrigue. Not everyone will celebrate your success." Antoine caught the warning, but it did not trouble him. To him, this was simply another stage, another game with new rules in a new land. And he was ready, ready to show the Russian court that he was not just a chef but a force of culinary brilliance, unlike anything they had ever seen.

Tsar Alexander I

Savior of Europe, Ruler of Contradictions

Antoine's first meeting with Tsar Alexander I came unexpectedly. As he toured the palace kitchens, a soft voice broke through.

"So, you are the man who turns sugar into cathedrals."

Antoine turned to see the Tsar standing in the doorway, his figure framed by the light streaming in behind him. Alexander's appearance was striking—tall and regal, with piercing blue eyes that seemed to look through a person rather than at them. His military uniform, though immaculate, bore none of the ostentation Antoine had seen among the courtiers. There was an air of calm authority about him but also a subtle restlessness, as though his mind was forever battling.

"Your Majesty, I am humbled to serve."

Alexander stepped closer to Antoine, "I have read about your work. They call you an artist, but here, you must also be a diplomat. This banquet is more than a meal; it is a symbol, a bridge between nations. Tell me, Monsieur Carême, do you believe art can achieve such things?"

Antoine face to face with the Tsar, his voice steady. "I do, Your Majesty. Art speaks where words fail. It can inspire, unify, and remind us of what is possible." A faint smile touched Alexander's lips. "Good. Then we understand one another."

As Antoine settled into the palace kitchens, he quickly noticed the undercurrents of tension that ran beneath the surface. The Russian cooks, though respectful, exchanged furtive glances as they worked alongside him. Rumors swirled through the palace corridors of alliances shifting, noble families vying for influence, and whispers that the French chef's presence was more than culinary.

As he toiled late into the evening, meticulously crafting, a flicker of movement near the kitchen door caught his eye. A lone figure lingered at the threshold, shrouded in darkness, his features concealed, yet his stance radiated quiet vigilance. Antoine kept his focus on the task at hand, his fingers deftly shaping fragile sugar petals, feigning obliviousness. But when he finally shifted his gaze to meet the intruder, the doorway stood eerily vacant.

The next morning, Vorontsov approached him with a grave expression. "You should know, Monsieur, that your success here has not gone unnoticed. There are those who see your presence as a threat, a reminder of France's influence in a court that prizes its autonomy."

In a calm, measured tone, Antoine replied, "I am here to create, not to contend. But rest assured, I understand your meaning."

"Intentions matter little in this city," Vorontsov replied. "St. Petersburg is a place where intense desire masks itself as friendship, and betrayal often wears a smile. Be vigilant."

The Pièce Montée: A Monument to Unity

For the banquet's centerpiece, Antoine designed a sugar replica of the Church of the Savior on Spilled Blood. Its vibrant onion domes would consist of marzipan in bold reds and greens, while its intricate facades were rendered in spun sugar. Standing nearly five feet tall, the pièce montée was a tribute to Russian architecture and a celebration of the unity promised by the treaty.

As the day of the banquet approached, Antoine worked tirelessly, his focus unyielding. The Russian cooks, once wary, now rallied around him, their admiration for his skill overcoming their initial reservations.

The banquet was a spectacle of grandeur. The grand hall of the Winter Palace shimmered with candlelight, its tables adorned with crystal and gold. Diplomats and nobility from across Europe mingled their conversations, a delicate dance of politics and power. When Antoine's pièce montée was unveiled, the room fell silent. The sugar cathedral stood as a masterpiece, its vivid colors and intricate details drawing gasps of admiration. Even the most stoic dignitaries broke into applause. Tsar Alexander rose, his expression one of quiet awe. "Monsieur Carême," he said, his voice carrying across the hall, "your creation is not merely a dessert. It is a testament to what is possible when skill meets vision. Russia thanks you."

"Your Majesty, it has been my greatest pleasure."

Yet, as the applause swelled, Antoine caught a familiar figure at the edge of the room; this time, their eyes met briefly before the figure melted into the crowd. Later that evening, as Antoine returned to his quarters, he found another letter slipped under his door. The paper was plain, the message stark:

"Beware the cost of brilliance. Even cathedrals can crumble."

Voiceover (Older Antoine):

"St. Petersburg was both a triumph and a warning. My work kept showing me the power of art to unite and inspire, but it also revealed the fragility of this art form. In the gilded halls of the Winter Palace, I learned that success is never without its shadows and that the higher you climb, the more carefully you must tread."

CHAPTER 18
RIVALS IN THE ROYAL COURT

Antoine Carême returned to Paris from St. Petersburg triumphant but wary. His pièce montée for Tsar Alexander I had garnered international acclaim, elevating his reputation to a height few chefs could dream of. Yet, with every success, Antoine felt the shadows around him lengthen. The sabotage he barely avoided in Paris, the veiled threats in St. Petersburg, and the whispers of bitterness all painted a clear picture: his rising star was both a beacon and a target.

The morning after his return, Talleyrand summoned him to his private study. The room was dimly lit, the faint scent of pipe smoke curling through the air. Antoine found the diplomat seated behind his desk, a letter bearing the royal crest of England spread before him. Talleyrand gestured for Antoine to sit, continuously fixed on the chef. "Chef Carême, it appears your artistry has caught the attention of another court. Prince Regent George IV has sent an invitation. He requests your presence to oversee the coronation banquet at Carlton House."

Antoine's breath caught. The Prince Regent—soon to be crowned King of England—was infamous for his indulgent lifestyle and love of grandeur. A coronation banquet for such a figure would be a spectacle unlike any other. It was an opportunity that could cement Antoine's legacy as Europe's premier chef.

"Your silence tells me you grasp the gravity of this offer,"Talleyrand continued, his tone measured. "But be warned. The English court is not like ours. Their politics are labyrinthine, their allegiances fleeting. And the Prince Regent... he is a man of insatiable appetites. He will demand all of you, and then he will demand more." Antoine's voice is steady despite the storm of emotions within. "I accept, Monseigneur. I will give England a banquet worthy of its new king."

Prince Regent George IV

A Portrait of Excess

As Antoine prepared for his journey to London, he read extensively about the Prince Regent. George IV, known for his flamboyant tastes and decadent lifestyle, had long been a controversial figure in British politics. His love of art, fashion, and fine cuisine had transformed Carlton House into a symbol of opulence, yet his extravagance often alienated the public. To some, he was a patron of culture; to others, a ruler out of touch with his people's struggles. Antoine knew he would need to navigate the prince's court carefully. George IV was not merely a ruler—he was a performer, and his coronation banquet would be a stage upon which his vision of English grandeur would be displayed.

Compared to the arduous trek to St. Petersburg, the journey to London felt brisk, but Antoine's anticipation was no less intense. Upon arriving at Carlton House, he was greeted by an incredible scene—servants darting through gilded halls, their arms laden with fine china, crystal goblets, and bolts of fabric for draping the banquet tables. The Prince Regent's steward, a stout man named Sir Edmund Haversham, greeted Antoine with a broad smile and a booming voice. "Monsieur Carême! Welcome to Carlton House. His Royal Highness has heard much of your talents and expects nothing short of genius."

Antoine inclined his head. "I will not disappoint."

Sir Edmund's face darkened as he leaned closer. "The Prince Regent is a man of… particular tastes. His favor is hard-earned and even harder to maintain. He surrounds himself with those who can amuse and impress him, but he has little patience for failure." As Antoine was led to the kitchens, he took in the disorganized chaos around him. English cooks glanced up from their stations, their expressions ranging from curiosity to thinly veiled hostility. It didn't take long for Antoine to realize that his arrival had upset the kitchen balance. The English head chef, a tall man with fiery red hair named Edward Mallory, greeted Antoine with a curt nod. His posture was stiff, his tone clipped. "So, you're the Frenchman who's come to teach us how to cook for our own king."

Antoine met Mallory's scrutiny evenly. "I am here to collaborate, not to teach." Mallory, with a little smirk, "Let us hope your reputation isn't exaggerated."

The tension was palpable, but Antoine chose not to rise to the bait. Instead, he surveyed the kitchen, quickly identifying areas of inefficiency. Over the next few hours, he set about establishing order, his quiet authority commanding the respect of most, if not all, the kitchen staff.

Yet Mallory remained an obstacle. He challenged Antoine at every turn, questioning his methods and dismissing his ideas. It was clear that Mallory viewed Antoine not as a colleague but as a threat.

For the coronation banquet, Antoine envisioned a pièce montée that would pay homage to English heritage while showcasing his signature mastery. Inspired by Stonehenge, he designed a towering sugar replica of the ancient monument, its arches, and pillars rendered in caramel and nougatine. Surrounding the structure were delicate sugar roses, symbolizing the Tudor lineage, and miniature pastilles depicting key moments in British history. The English cooks watched in awe as Antoine worked, their initial skepticism giving way to admiration. Even Mallory, despite his scorn, couldn't hide his grudging respect for Antoine's exactness and vision.

Court Intrigue Unfolds

As the banquet drew closer, Antoine couldn't ignore the sense of disquiet that floated in the air. Whispers of discontent echoed through the palace corridors. Mallory, emboldened by his resentment, began sowing seeds of doubt among the staff, claiming that Antoine's French flair would overshadow English tradition.

One evening, as Antoine worked on the pièce montée, he noticed Mallory near his station. The red-haired chef's discriminations held more than disdain; it was calculation. Antoine feigned indifference but doubled his vigilance, knowing that Mallory's envy could turn dangerous. Antoine was no stranger to all the dangers that were brought about by his success.

Misfortune struck on the eve of the banquet. Antoine stepped into the kitchen, the familiar scent of caramelized sugar and warm pastry filling the air, only to be met with a sight that made his stomach twist. His grand sugar sculpture, the crowning glory of the evening's display—lay in ruins. Shattered arches of spun sugar, once delicate and majestic, were now jagged fragments scattered across the marble worktable. Fine dust from crushed pastillage clung to the air, and the centerpiece that had taken days of meticulous work was reduced to wreckage.

His pulse quickened, but he did not allow himself to panic. He had learned long ago that disaster was an inevitable companion in the competitive world of the royal kitchens. He had faced fire, theft, and sabotage before—this was no different. His eyes swept over the destruction, his mind already reconstructing the piece, but first, he needed answers. "Who did this?" Antoine's voice, though quiet, carried the weight of command. Cold, sharp, unwavering. The kitchen fell silent. The other cooks hesitated, their eyes darting to one another, searching for a scapegoat or an excuse. No one spoke. Some looked away; others busied themselves with their work. In the farthest corner of the room, Mallory stood motionless, arms crossed, his expression unreadable. Antoine's gaze lingered on him for a moment before shifting back to the rest of the room.

Before anyone could muster a response, Sir Edmund stormed into the kitchen, his powdered wig slightly askew, his usually composed demeanor cracked with fury. "This is sabotage!" he bellowed, his voice echoing off the stone walls. "Monsieur Carême, can the centerpiece be salvaged?" Antoine straightened, brushing the sugar dust from his sleeves. His jaw was set, his dark eyes burning with quiet determination. "It can," he said firmly. "And it will."

There was no room for doubt, no space for fear. His reputation had been built on precision, resilience, and brilliance under pressure. He would not fail now—not when the eyes of the most powerful men in Europe would soon feast upon his art. The kitchen remained still for a breath, and then, without another word, Antoine rolled up his sleeves. The battle was not lost. The masterpiece would rise again.

The Banquet's Triumph

Despite another setback, Antoine worked tirelessly through the night, his hands moving with relentless precision. The kitchen had long since fallen silent, the other cooks retreating to their beds, but he remained, a lone figure in the candlelight, sculpting, molding, breathing life back into what had been destroyed. There was no room for doubt, no time for exhaustion. His vision would not be broken. By the time the first rays of dawn filtered through the kitchen windows, the masterpiece stood once more. Stronger. More refined. Unbreakable.

That evening, as the grand doors of the banquet hall swung open, a collective gasp rippled through the gathered nobility. There, standing beneath the dancing glow of a hundred chandeliers, was Antoine's sugar Stonehenge, a spectacle of delicate grandeur, its arches rising in perfect symmetry, the crystalline glint of caramel and pastillage mimicking the weathered stones of its namesake. It defied destruction, a monument to his craft and defiance. Prince Regent George IV pushed back his chair and rose to his feet, his eyes alight with astonishment. He lifted his goblet high, the jewels on his fingers catching the light. "Magnificent!" he proclaimed, his voice rich with admiration. "Monsieur Carême, this is no mere confection. It is a conquest worthy of kings, worthy of this moment in history. England owes you its gratitude."

Antoine inclined his head, his features composed, but beneath the measured response, "Thank you, Your Royal Highness", a much deeper satisfaction burned. He had reclaimed what was his. The room swelled with admiration, voices rising in awe as courtiers pressed closer to marvel at the details, the delicate engravings, and the near-translucent fineness of the sugar work. Yet, amid the praise, Antoine's sharp eyes caught a movement in the periphery. A shadow slipped through the crowd.

Mallory.

The red-haired chef's face was rigid with barely contained fury, his jaw tight, his fists curled at his sides. He did not stop to admire the sculpture, nor did he meet Antoine's gaze. Instead, he disappeared through a side door, swallowed by the darkness beyond. Antoine watched him go, his own expression unreadable. Victory had been claimed tonight. But the war was far from over.

Voiceover (Older Antoine):

"The coronation banquet was a triumph, but triumphs rarely come without a price. With every admirer I won, a rival emerged in equal measure. Success was a double-edged blade, capable of elevating me to greatness but just as easily turning against me if I failed to wield it with caution. I was becoming accustomed, with each passing day, to the delicate art of survival in the kitchens, where ambition was as sharp as any knife, and only the most cunning could truly flourish."

The following morning, as he stepped into the kitchen, his gaze dropped to the floor. There, just beneath his door, lay a folded slip of parchment. He already knew what it was before he even bent to retrieve it. By now, it had become a pattern, one that tested Antoine's patience as much as his resolve. Another note. Another silent intrusion. How many times had this happened? Too many. Each message was short, calculated, and unsettling. Was it a mere game, an attempt to rattle his focus, to keep him looking over his shoulder? Or was it something more? A warning? A prelude to something far worse, something beyond sabotage? His fingers tightened around the parchment as he unfolded it.

The message was simple—but chilling.

"Beware the envy of those who walk beside you. Not all daggers are drawn in the open."

Antoine folded the note carefully; he had survived court intrigue in Paris and St. Petersburg, and he would do so again in London. His oeuvre was his voice and weapon, and he would wield it with unyielding precision.

CHAPTER 19
SUGAR, PAPER, AND DIPLOMACY

The journey back to Paris from London felt both victorious and sobering for Antoine Carême. The coronation banquet for Prince Regent George IV had been a dazzling success, yet it came with a heavy reminder: the heights of success were perilous. The destruction of his pièce montée in Carlton House's kitchens remained in his mind, a bitter echo of the rivalry that seemed to follow him from kitchen to kitchen, palace to palace, country to country.

Still, the acclaim he received in England brought him even closer to the immortality he sought—not merely fame but a legacy. Paris greeted him as a hero, his reputation now as much a subject of admiration as of envy. Requests poured in from every corner of the city, each demanding creations pushing culinary art's boundaries. Yet Antoine found himself increasingly restless. The fleeting approval of nobles no longer satisfied him. He craved permanence.

A Seed of Legacy

As sunlight poured through the windows of Talleyrand's estate kitchen, Antoine stood over a table littered with sketches for his next création incroyable. Inspired by the Louvre's neoclassical façade, he envisioned a towering creation of nougatine columns and spun sugar pediments. Yet, even as he sketched the intricate details, his thoughts wandered to the question that had begun to haunt him: *What will endure when the applause fades?* His musings were interrupted by a familiar voice. "Still chasing perfection, I see."

Antoine turned to find Hélène standing in the doorway, her mischievous smile tempered by an unmistakable warmth. She carried a small leather-bound notebook and set it on the table before him.

"What's this?" Antoine asked, his curiosity piqued.

Hélène gestured for him to open it. Inside, Antoine found transcribed notes on his pièce montées, recipes, and even technical details of his sugar work. Each page was illustrated with sketches—some his own, others clearly rendered by Hélène.

"I've been keeping track," Hélène said softly. "Your work deserves to be more than a memory. It should be studied and shared. You should write a book, Antoine. A codex of your achievements."

Antoine closed the notebook. "A book? But my work is meant to be experienced, not merely described on a page."

Hélène's look held steady. "And how many will get to experience it? A book can travel farther than you ever will. It can inspire chefs long after you're gone. Isn't that the legacy you've been searching for?" What she said struck a chord Antoine hadn't known was there. The idea of preserving his existence in writing, of creating something that would endure long after his hands could no longer form sugar and dough, planted itself firmly in his mind.

Voiceover (Older Antoine):

"Hélène's suggestion was like a window thrown open in a stifling room. Until then, I had thought of my work as ephemeral—moments of beauty meant to be savored and forgotten. But the thought of creating something lasting, something that could transcend the limits of time, began to consume me."

The Congress of Vienna

Some days later, Talleyrand summoned Antoine to his study. The diplomat's sharpness betrayed none of the tension that usually accompanied his summons, but his tone was deliberate. "Antoine," Talleyrand began, "France is preparing for an international congress in Vienna. Leaders from across Europe will convene to determine the future of the continent. I need you to lead the culinary efforts for the French delegation."

Antoine's pulse hastened. The Congress of Vienna was more than a diplomatic gathering; it was the stage upon which nations displayed their power and culture. Every detail, from the negotiations to the banquets, would be scrutinized. His work would not just represent him—it would represent France.

"This is a performance, not just a meal," Talleyrand continued. "Your oeuvre d'art will speak as loudly as any treaty. Show them that France's culture remains unparalleled."

His voice was steady, but his mind raced. "I will give them something unforgettable. But who will strike next, as they have so many times before? No matter—I'll be ready."

Antoine set out for Vienna accompanied by a caravan of ingredients, tools, and a handpicked team of cooks. The journey was long and arduous, but he used the time to refine and perfect. Inspired by France's cultural and architectural heritage, he envisioned a pièce montée that would symbolize unity and resilience: a towering sugar sculpture of the Arc de Triomphe adorned with depictions of French philosophers, composers, and revolutionaries.

As the French delegation arrived in Vienna, they were greeted by a city brimming with both opulence and tension. The Congress of Vienna was a gathering of power brokers, each vying to assert their nation's influence. Antoine understood that his chef-d'oeuvre was not just a dessert—it was a statement of France's place in this fragile new order.

Vienna's Court Intrigue

The palace kitchens in Vienna buzzed with energy as cooks from various delegations worked side by side. Antoine's arrival caused a stir, his reputation preceding him even here. Yet, alongside the admiration, he sensed the currents of rivalry and intrigue.

The Austrian head chef, Klaus Richter, greeted Antoine with polite formality. But beneath the surface, Antoine detected a hint of tension. "You have quite the reputation, Monsieur Carême," Klaus said, his tone measured. "It will be interesting to see how your French flair fits into this… diplomatic setting."

Antoine smiled faintly. "Food speaks a universal language, Chef Richter. I hope my work will contribute to the harmony of this gathering." Antoine had become highly adept in the language of the kitchen and the intricate dance of its politics. Klaus, with a slight head tilt, his smile struggling to reach his eyes.

As the days wore on, Antoine noticed subtle attempts to undermine him: misplaced tools, spoiled ingredients, and whispers among the staff. It was clear and expected that not everyone would welcome the idea of France asserting itself so boldly through its cuisine.

A common warning echoed in his mind: *Trust no one completely.*

The sun dipped below the horizon, painting the sky in a symphony of gold and crimson as if whispering a final, tender farewell to the day. The Congress's grand banquet had arrived, and it was a spectacle of diplomacy and decadence. Chandeliers bathed the hall in golden light, illuminating tables set with fine china and crystal. At the center of the room stood Antoine's pièce montée: the Arc de Triomphe rendered in gleaming sugar, its arches adorned with intricate patterns of spun sugar and nougatine. Around its base, sugar figurines depicted Voltaire, Rousseau, and other French luminaries.

As the banquet began, diplomats and royals alike marveled at Antoine's creation. Even Klaus Richter, though reluctant, acknowledged its magnificence.

Talleyrand approached Antoine, his expression one of rare approval. "You have done France proud tonight, Carême. Your work has reminded me that while others may hold power, we hold culture."

Antoine stood taller, a deep sense of accomplishment roaring from within. "Thank you, Monseigneur."

Voiceover (Older Antoine): *"The Congress of Vienna was a turning point—not just for Europe, but for me. It was one of the few times I fully realized the power of my abilities. My work was identity, diplomacy, and defiance. It spoke in a language that transcended borders and politics."*

As the delegation made its final preparations to depart Vienna, a courier arrived bearing a letter sealed with the Austrian imperial crest. The weight of the parchment alone spoke of its importance. Antoine broke the seal, his eyes scanning the elegant script within. It was an invitation. An offer to remain in Vienna as the head chef to Emperor Francis I. A prestigious position, one that would grant him unparalleled influence, security, and the ear of an empire.

For a moment, he allowed himself to consider it. The grandeur of the Habsburg court, the endless feasts, the challenge of shaping imperial cuisine. It was tempting. But deep in his soul, he knew his heart belonged to Paris. He declined the offer with grace, penning his response with steady hands. Gratitude, admiration, respect, but no hesitation. His path was clear. When he returned to France, the familiar streets of Paris embraced him like an old friend. The scent of fresh bread drifting from boulangeries, the murmur of poets and revolutionaries in cafés, the Seine flowing like a ribbon of silver through the heart of the city—this was home. And there was someone he needed to see.

That evening, beneath the soft glow of streetlamps, Antoine sought out Hélène at their usual meeting place along the riverbank. The city's lights reflected on the water, dancing in golden ripples as a warm breeze carried the scent of blooming jasmine. She was already there, waiting, the lambent lamplight catching the gentle curve of her smile. Without a word, he handed her the notebook she had given him months ago. It was no longer empty. The once-pristine pages were now filled—sketches of towering sugar sculptures, detailed notes on flavors and techniques, recipes refined through fire and experience. Hélène traced her fingers over the inked pages before looking up at him. Antoine met her gaze, his voice firm, unwavering. "You were right. It's time to write my story." A slow, radiant smile spread across her lips. "Our world will be better for it, Antoine."

They walked along the Seine, the soft rhythm of their footsteps blending with the distant hum of the city. The weight of courts, rivalries, and expectations had defined so much of his life. But now, for the first time in months, he felt truly free. He had dazzled kings, reshaped culinary artistry, and conquered the most ruthless kitchens in Europe. But his greatest work was still ahead of him. His legacy would not only be carved in sugar and butter but in ink—a testament to the art, the passion, and the relentless pursuit of perfection that had defined his life.

PART V
THE EXPANDING
FLAME

CHAPTER 20
A RISING TIDE

ntoine Carême returned to Paris from Vienna with a sense of joy tempered by an unwavering resolve. The Congress of Vienna had been a success, and his pièce montée, a breathtaking sugar Arc de Triomphe—stood as a symbol of France's enduring culinary supremacy. Yet, even as he basked in his accomplishments, he remained watchful. The whispers of envy and intrigue had followed him from one grand kitchen to the next, and he had learned that success came at a cost. This time, he would not be caught off guard.

Paris embraced him as a hero. Nobles clamored for his presence, salons overflowed with discussions of his latest triumph, and newspapers lauded him as a national treasure. But beneath the admiration, Antoine sensed something else: expectation, pressure, and a hunger to see what he would create next. He could not simply succeed; he had to surpass himself repeatedly, and he had to find out who had been working against him all along.

One morning, Antoine arrived at Talleyrand's estate to find the kitchen brimming with restless energy. Dupont, the ever-watchful chef, handed him a letter sealed with an unfamiliar crest. "This came for you," Dupont said, his gaze unreadable. "An invitation from the royal court of Bavaria."

Antoine broke the seal and read the elegant script. The King of Bavaria sought his talents for a grand celebration, a banquet to honor a new royal alliance. It was an opportunity to spread his influence further, beyond Vienna, beyond St. Petersburg, beyond even Paris itself. But it would also serve another purpose. Antoine set the letter down and met Dupont's gaze. "This trip will be different." Dupont, with a curious look on his face, "How so?"

"Because this time, I refuse to simply wait for the next attack. I intend to set a trap, one that will finally unmask whoever has been behind the notes, the sabotages, the relentless attempts to see me undone. This is no mere rival acting out of petty jealousy. No, this is someone with influence, someone with reach. Someone who has followed me from court to court, striking from the shadows. But no more. They believe they are untouchable, hidden behind whispers and careful hands. I will make them step into the light. And when they do, they will find that I am ready." I have been fortunate, each act of sabotage, each attempt to destroy my work, I have managed to undo. I have salvaged, rebuilt, and restored my creations time and time again. But it is that very success that troubles me the most. Whoever is behind this must be seething. Every failure to ruin me only fuels their hatred further. If their intent was to break my spirit, to force me into submission, then my resilience has only driven them to greater desperation. And that is what worries me.

This is someone with a purpose, someone who will not stop until I am no more. They have persisted through every setback, every foiled attempt. If they have not stopped thus far, what makes you think they ever will?

A Game of Shadows

In the weeks leading up to the Bavarian commission, Antoine meticulously laid out his plans. He had grown accustomed to the anonymous notes, the whispers, the sabotage that had followed him across Europe. Someone was determined to see him fail, but he had never been able to catch them in the act or discover who it was.

Until now.

He carefully selected a small team from Talleyrand's kitchen, including several cooks he suspected might be involved or, at the very least, knew more than they let on. He let slip false rumors about a secret ingredient, a technique only he knew, something so vital to the Bavarian banquet that its absence would spell disaster.

Then, he waited.

The journey to Bavaria was filled with the usual tension, the weight of expectation. But Antoine's thoughts were elsewhere. He was watching, listening. Studying the subtle movements of those around him. One of them would make a mistake. Upon arriving at the Bavarian royal palace, Antoine was greeted with skepticism by the head chef, a burly man named Otto. "We've heard much about you, Monsieur Carême," Otto said gruffly. "But let's see if your skills live up to the tales." Antoine brushed off the comment as he was used to hearing those exact words from kitchen to kitchen. Antoine wasted no time. He reorganized the kitchen with military precision, his commands slicing through the language barrier. His pièce montée—a sugar cathedral, its delicate spires reaching for the heavens—would be the crown jewel of the banquet. Every detail had to be perfect. And then, on the eve of the banquet, it happened.

A shadow slipped into the kitchen long after the fires had burned low. Moving swiftly, cautiously. The saboteur approached the table where the fragile sugar masterpiece stood, their hand reaching for the carefully sculpted spire.

"Step away."

The voice was calm and controlled, but it cut through the darkness like a blade. The figure froze. A heartbeat of hesitation, then a lunge, but hands caught them before they could flee. The torches flared to life, revealing the culprit.

Mallory.

The red-haired chef who had followed Antoine from court to court, always watching from the shadows, always resentful. He had been the one behind the notes, the subtle acts of sabotage. The one who had sought to unravel Antoine's legacy from within. Antoine stepped forward, his expression unreadable. "How long, Mallory?" he asked quietly. "How long have you been waiting for me to fail?" Mallory's eyes pierced. "Since the day you stepped into Talleyrand's kitchen. You were nothing, a nobody, yet you rose above us all. No matter where you went, no matter how many times I tried to stop you, you kept rising." Antoine studied him for a long moment, then exhaled slowly.

Antoine had always dismissed the strange meeting in the café as an odd encounter, a man who claimed to be a 'facilitator of influence' speaking in cryptic riddles. At the time, it had seemed little more than an eccentric conversation, a veiled warning he couldn't quite decipher. But now, standing before Mallory, watching the anger scorching behind his former colleague's eyes, Antoine began to see the pieces align. Mallory had been following him long before England, long before the notes. Long before the first sugar sculpture had been shattered, this wasn't the work of a bitter rival who had simply decided to act out; it had been planned and orchestrated. Why? Antoine studied him carefully.

"You weren't acting alone, were you?"

Mallory's sneer deepened. "You think you're so clever, Carême. You think the world has been yours for the taking. But you never stopped to question how many wanted to see you fall."

"And who exactly are they?"

Mallory chuckled darkly. "Does it matter? Would you even understand?"

The words struck Antoine as a deflection—a lie wrapped in arrogance. He had seen men like Mallory before, proud, self-righteous, unwilling to admit their weaknesses. Mallory would rather paint himself as a soldier in some unseen war than confess that, in the end, his own envy and insecurities had driven him to destruction. But still, the café encounter lingered in his mind. Had Mallory been recruited by someone? Or had he used others to further his own hatred?

Antoine narrowed his gaze. "The man I met in the café, the one who spoke of influence, of unseen hands pulling strings. Who was he to you? A lackey? A benefactor? Had he hired you and Julien, or were you behind it all? Was Jacques involved? He always seemed to always know what was going on before I did, the bearer of bad news.

For the first time, a flicker of something crossed Mallory's expression. Hesitation? Amusement? Fear? It was impossible to tell. But Antoine knew it was impossible that Mallory had not been acting entirely alone. Perhaps he had been the mastermind of the sabotage. Perhaps he had given the orders, written the notes, and orchestrated the moments where Antoine's success was nearly undone.

But someone else—some unseen force—had given him the means.

"Was it money?" Antoine asked quietly. "Or did they simply whisper in your ear, feed your jealousy, give you a reason to justify it all?"

Mallory's jaw clenched, his silence more telling than words.

Antoine is trying to calm himself.

"I don't need to know the names," he said at last. "Because in the end, none of them matter. You did this. You let this consume you."

Mallory's face twisted in rage. "And yet, here you stand, unscathed. The untouchable Carême."

Antoine shook his head. "Not untouched. Just unwilling to be devoured by the same darkness that took you."

As the guards dragged Mallory away, Antoine felt a strange sense of closure but not certainty. Whoever the man in the café and storage room had been, he had not shown himself again. Antoine would never know if Mallory had been merely a pawn in someone else's game or if he had used the power of unseen benefactors for his own twisted purpose.

But in the end, it no longer mattered.

The real enemy, the one who had haunted his steps and who had tried to break him, was no longer in the shadows. Antoine had won, and now he was free from the overhanging darkness.

Voiceover (Older Antoine):

"I could never understand Mallory's actions—not truly. The sabotage, the relentless pursuit to see me fail, the notes left in the dark, the careful, calculated destruction of my work. What could drive a man to dedicate himself not to creation but to its ruin? But I have come to realize that jealousy, envy, and insecurity are poisons that seep deep into the soul. Left unchecked, they do not merely linger; they consume. They twist ambition into resentment, admiration into hatred. Mallory was not just trying to stop me—he was trying to fill the void inside himself, one that no amount of sabotage could ever satisfy. And in the end, he was not the one who truly suffered. It was his own obsession that devoured him, leaving nothing behind but bitterness and regret."

Hélène's Vision

Upon returning to Paris, Antoine sought out Hélène. They met at their usual spot by the Seine, the city's lights casting golden ripples across the water. The city was alive with murmurs of his latest feat, but for the first time in a long while, Antoine felt no urgency to chase the next one. Hélène greeted him with a knowing smile. "Another victory, I hear," she said, her voice warm with pride. "Bavaria must be buzzing with your name." Antoine exhaled, turning the medal over in his palm before pressing it into her hand. "The banquet was a success," he admitted. "And more importantly, I caught the man behind the sabotage. It's over, Hélène. Whoever was pulling the strings, Mallory or otherwise, they failed. I can finally breathe." She studied him, her fingers tracing the edges of the medal. "And yet, you don't look relieved."

Antoine gave a quiet chuckle, though there was little humor in it. "Because it doesn't feel like I thought it would." He paused, watching the lights on the river's surface. "I thought once I uncovered the truth and removed the threat, I'd feel... victorious. But all I feel is tired. As if every success only leaves behind a greater emptiness." Hélène's expression softened, her eyes full of understanding. "Perhaps that's because you've been measuring success the wrong way." Antoine turned to her, listening.

"You have spent your life proving yourself to kings, rivals, and those who doubted you. And you have won, Antoine. Again and again." She reached for his hand. "But what happens when there's no longer a need to prove? When the rivalries end, the applause fades? What remains?"

Antoine hesitated.

Hélène smiled, the corners of her eyes crinkling with warmth. "Your work is already admired, but if you want it to last, you must put it to paper." Antoine's eyes looked to the ground. "What if it fails? What if no one cares to read it?" Hélène's grip on his hand tightened. "Then you've lost nothing. But if it succeeds, you will have given something no one can take away. Your legacy, preserved." A spark ignited within him, not the frenzied hunger to create for others, impress, outdo, but something deeper, something lasting. For years, he had built ephemeral monuments—sugar, flour, fire, and ice, all crafted to dazzle and disappear. But now, for the first time, he saw the book not as a distraction but as the culmination of everything he had fought for. It would be his voice, story, and gift to the future.

Antoine began immersing himself in the painstaking process of documenting his life's work. With Hélène's guidance, he filled page after page, recipes carefully transcribed, sketches meticulously drawn, techniques articulated with precision. The ink stained his fingers, and the candlelight burned late into the night, but he felt more alive than he had in years. Meanwhile, Paris still clamored for his talents, but Antoine chose his commissions carefully. No longer chasing prestige, he sought only those projects that refined his vision that reinforced his belief in his craft. He realized then that his life would not be defined by rivalries or sabotage, by the fleeting approval of kings or courtiers. It would not be a momentary triumph that faded with the next celebration. It would be written. A story etched in sugar and ink meant to endure long after the last banquet had been served. For now, Antoine chose to set aside his writing as his thoughts turned toward something even greater, a vision that extended beyond the pages of a book, something that could leave an even deeper mark on the world.

CHAPTER 21
A PALACE OF SWEETNESS

The idea had been simmering in Antoine's mind for months before he started writing, evolving from a vague thought to a fully realized vision. It was more than a dream; it was a declaration of purpose. After years of crafting fugacious masterpieces for kings and diplomats, Antoine longed for something permanent, something that would belong not only to the aristocracy but to all of Paris.

The concept crystallized after his return from Vienna, where the Congress had further solidified his belief in the unifying power of food. In his travels, Antoine had seen how his creations could bridge cultures and inspire awe. Now, he wanted to build a sanctuary of sensations—a place where anyone could experience the magic of culinary excellence.

Paris, with its hunger for beauty and innovation, was ready for something extraordinary. Antoine envisioned a pâtisserie unlike any other, a palace of sweetness where the boundaries between cuisine, art, and architecture would disappear. It would be called *La Maison de Sucre*, 'The House of Sugar'.

One crisp morning, Antoine stood in a quiet courtyard near the Seine, surveying an empty lot that would soon become the home of his grand vision. Hélène was at his side, her eyes sparkling with excitement as she took in the scene. "This will be your masterpiece," Hélène said, her voice steady yet filled with wonder. "A place where your legacy will flourish." A rare smile broke across his face. "Not mine alone," he said softly. "This will belong to Paris, to everyone who believes in the beauty of creation." Hélène tilted her head, studying him. "Have you decided what you'll call it?" Antoine hesitated, then spoke with quiet conviction. "La Maison de Sucre." The name seemed to carry weight even as he spoke it. Hélène's smile widened. "It's perfect."

The months that followed were marked by relentless energy and fervent endeavors. Architects and artisans worked tirelessly to bring Antoine's vision to life. He was deeply involved in every detail of the design, from the curvature of the windows to the patterns on the marble floors. The pâtisserie would echo the elegance of a grand salon, with gilded accents, tall windows that bathed the space in natural light, and a central atrium where guests could marvel at towering sugar sculptures. The kitchen was no less impressive, a state-of-the-art workspace outfitted with the latest tools, ample counter space, and ovens designed to accommodate the complexity of Antoine's creations. It was here that Antoine planned to train the next generation of chefs, passing down the techniques and philosophies that had propelled him to greatness.

He hired a team of skilled apprentices and cooks, each carefully chosen for their passion and precision. Several young talents who reminded Antoine of his own beginnings. Dupont, his former mentor, even paid a rare visit during the construction. "You've built something extraordinary," Dupont said, his usual husky voice betraying a hint of excitement for Antoine.

The Grand Opening

The opening of *La Maison de Sucre* was a spectacle Paris had never seen before. Crowds gathered outside, jostling for a glimpse of the pâtisserie that had been the talk of the city. Nobles and commoners alike filled the space, their expressions full of wonder as they took in the opulence around them.

The centerpiece of the opening was a breathtaking sugar replica of Notre Dame Cathedral, its spires reaching skyward and its façade adorned with intricate details rendered in caramel and nougatine.

Surrounding it were rows of miniature pastries arranged like a blooming garden, each one a testament to Antoine's meticulousness.

Talleyrand was among the first to arrive, scanning the room before settling on Antoine. "You've outdone yourself," he said, his tone unusually warm. "Paris will speak of this for decades." Antoine inclined his head. "Thank you, Monseigneur. Your guidance has always been invaluable."

As the day unfolded, Antoine moved through the crowd, his heart swelling with pride at the sight of people savoring his creations. Hélène joined him, a glass of champagne in her hand. "They love it," she said, her smile radiant. "You've given Paris something to believe in."

Antoine met her fix, his voice soft but resolute. "We've given Paris something to believe in."

Voiceover (Older Antoine):

"La Maison de Sucre was more than a pâtisserie. It was a dream realized, a space where art and taste converged with moments of joy. It stood as a testament to what could be achieved with vision, perseverance, and the belief that beauty could transform all."

The months that followed cemented *La Maison de Sucre* as a beacon of culinary innovation. Chefs from across Europe traveled to learn from Antoine, eager to master his techniques and understand his philosophy. His creations became symbols of Parisian excellence, their elegance whispered about in royal courts and bustling markets alike. Yet, for Antoine, the greatest reward was not the accolades or the fame. It was the sight of a child pressing their face against the glass, hypnotized with all their amazement at the sugary masterpieces inside. It was the laughter of friends sharing a tart, the quiet satisfaction of a worker savoring a pastry after a long day. It was the knowledge that his work brought joy, however fleeting, to the harshness that encompassed us.

One evening, as Antoine watched the city from the windows of *La Maison de Sucre*, Hélène sitting next to him, her hand slipping into his. "Do you think it will last?" she asked softly. Antoine smiled as he viewed the twinkling lights of Paris. "As long as there are those who believe in the power of creation, it will last."

The chef of kings had found his kingdom, built not of stone but of sugar and imagination. And in that kingdom, every creation was a reminder of the fire that had driven him, from the boy who worked in a small, simple bakery to the man who redefined the boundaries of culinary art.

Antoine Carême had conquered the courts of Europe, but it was in this palace of sweetness, surrounded by the people of Paris, that he truly felt like a king.

Voiceover (Older Antoine):

"Every sculpture, every pastry, every moment of wonder—it was all part of the legacy I wished to leave behind. In La Maison de Sucre, I found not just a home for my work but a home for my dreams. And in that, I found something even greater: a way to share the beauty of creation."

CHAPTER 22
THE BITTER AND THE SWEET

The years following the triumphant opening of *La Maison de Sucre* were full of creativity, acclaim, and growth for Antoine Carême. The pâtisserie stood as a jewel in Paris, a place where artistry met indulgence, drawing admirers from every corner of society. Each creation that emerged from its gilded halls was a story, a masterpiece that captured the imagination of nobles and commoners alike. Yet even as Antoine's dream flourished, a growing tension beneath the surface. The relentless pursuit of perfection, which had fueled his rise, now began to exact its toll.

Long after the last customers had departed and the pâtisserie was cloaked in quiet, Hélène found Antoine in the kitchen. He sat hunched over a half-finished design for a *pièce montée*, his head resting heavily in his hand. The marble counter was scattered with sketches and tools, the remnants of another long day. "You've been working too hard," Hélène said softly, setting a steaming cup of tea beside him. Her tone was gentle but firm. "Even you need to rest."

Antoine looked up, his face shadowed with exhaustion. He managed a faint smile of gratitude. "Rest feels like a luxury I cannot afford. There's always another creation, another challenge." Hélène pulled up a stool beside him, her gaze once again steady. "Antoine, you've already given so much. *La Maison de Sucre* is a marvel. You don't need to prove anything to anyone." Antoine sighed, running a hand through his hair. "It's not about proving anything. It's about creating something that endures, something that outlives me." Hélène placed a hand over his. "It already has. And it will, long after we're gone. But you can't carry on alone. Let others help; that is one of the reasons you create the school." Filling the spaces between the soft purr of the night were her words. For a moment, Antoine allowed himself to breathe, her presence a balm against the weight he carried.

Voiceover (Older Antoine):

"In those days, I was driven by an energy that refused to dim. I saw every moment of rest as a lost opportunity; every pan used as a delay. What I failed to understand was that even the fiercest flames needed tending, or they would burn out."

The strain on Antoine's health became undeniable while preparing for an ambitious commission. A wealthy patron, enamored with *La Maison de Sucre's* reputation, had requested a grand banquet to celebrate his daughter's wedding. The task was monumental: a sprawling sugar garden complete with chocolate fountains, marzipan sculptures of mythical creatures, and a centerpiece *pièce montée* depicting a fairytale castle. Antoine approached the project with his usual intensity, pouring every ounce of energy into the designs and execution. He spent countless nights refining the details, the glow of the kitchen lamps often the only light in the building. His team worked tirelessly under his direction, their admiration for his vision tempered by concern for his well-being.

Hélène, too, watched with growing restlessness. "Antoine," she urged one evening, "you need to take a step back. Let your team carry more of the load." But Antoine was unyielding. "This is my responsibility," he replied. "They're counting on me."

The day of the banquet arrived, and the sugar garden was unveiled to rapturous applause. Guests marveled at the intricate details, their faces alight with wonder as they wandered through the edible marvel. The centerpiece castle gleamed under the chandeliers, it's sweet spires stretching to new heights. Yet, as the accolades poured in, Antoine stood at the edge of the room, gripping the back of a chair for support. His face was pale, his breath shallow. Hélène was at his side in an instant. "Antoine," she whispered urgently, her voice filled with worry, "you need to stop." "I'm fine," he insisted, though his voice lacked conviction. "Their expectations of me will never cease." "They'll understand," Hélène said firmly, guiding him toward a quieter corner. "Your health matters more than their applause."

For the first time in years, Antoine allowed himself to step away. He watched as his team carried on seamlessly, their efforts reflecting the lessons he had imparted. It was an overwhelming realization and one that would shape the path ahead.

The days that followed marked a turning point. Antoine began to delegate responsibilities with greater trust, relinquishing tasks he had once guarded fiercely. To his surprise, his apprentices rose to the occasion, their work imbued with the precision and care he had instilled in them. *La Maison de Sucre* continued to thrive, its reputation growing as a center of innovation and excellence. Antoine, meanwhile, found a new rhythm, one that allowed him to savor moments he had once overlooked. Quiet evenings with Hélène, the laughter of his team, the sight of a child's face lighting up at the sight of their first macaron, these became the treasures of his days.

Voiceover (Older Antoine):

"I had always believed that my work defined me, that my worth was measured by the creations I left behind. But as the years passed, I came to see that my true legacy was not in sugar and flour, but in the people I had touched, the joy I had brought, and the lessons I had shared."

One evening, as the sun dipped below the horizon and the lights of Paris began to twinkle, Antoine and Hélène stood on the balcony of their apartment. Below them, *La Maison de Sucre* glowed warmly, its windows alive with laughter and light. "Do you ever regret any of it?" Hélène asked, her voice soft but curious. Antoine's smile was faint and faraway yet suffused with quiet contentment. "No. Every challenge, every triumph, every moment brought me here. And here is enough." Hélène slipped her hand into his, her touch grounding him. Together, they watched the city that had shaped their lives, its heartbeat steady and enduring.

Voiceover (Older Antoine):

"In the end, I found that success was not in the applause or the accolades but in the quiet satisfaction of knowing I had found something meaningful. My fire had burned dazzlingly, not for myself, but for those who had shared in its warmth."

Antoine Carême had reached the pinnacle of his art, his name synonymous with excellence. Yet it was not the grand banquets or the accolades that defined him in those final years. It was the simple moments of joy, continuing to watch young apprentices find their stride, seeing a family share a dessert, and hearing the laughter that filled the halls of *La Maison de Sucre*. He had built more than a pâtisserie. He had built a world of inspiration, a reminder that beauty and creation could touch even the hardest people. And in that legacy, Antoine Carême found his peace.

CHAPTER 23
THE LEGACY TAKES SHAPE

The year was 1825, a time of profound transformation in France. The Bourbon monarchy sought to restore stability, but the undercurrents of revolution and reform simmered beneath the surface. Paris itself was a city caught between its past grandeur and an uncertain future; its streets were alive with the energy of possibility. Amid this backdrop, Antoine Carême found himself at a crossroads. His fame had reached its zenith, yet his thoughts turned increasingly toward the future—not just his own, but that of what he had helped shape.

One crisp autumn afternoon, Antoine and Hélène strolled along the banks of the Marne. The buzzing with life around them: merchants hawking wares, children laughing, and the distant clatter of horse-drawn carriages. As they walked, Antoine was drawn to a street vendor's modest cart laden with pastries. The vendor's tarts and biscuits were simple, yet a small crowd had gathered. Children giggled as they shared a flaky pastry, and adults murmured their appreciation over delicate bites. Hélène noticed Antoine's expression soften as he watched the scene. "Do you miss those days?" she asked gently. Antoine smiled faintly, his hands clasped behind his back. "Sometimes. There's a purity in simplicity—a direct connection between the creator and the people. It's something I've tried to preserve, even in my most elaborate work. But I wonder if I've succeeded." Hélène slipped her arm through his, her tone warm and encouraging. "You have. That's what sets you apart. You've never forgotten where you began." The street vendor's scene etched in his mind as they continued their walk. It was a reminder of the joy that could be found in the simplest of creations, a joy he hoped to pass on.

That evening, Antoine gathered his closest apprentices in the kitchen of *La Maison de Sucre*. The glow of the lamps cast long shadows on the walls, and quiet anticipation filled the air. For weeks, he had been contemplating a project that combined his expertise with his growing desire to preserve and expand his lifelong love.

"I've spent my life creating," Antoine began, his voice steady and deliberate. "But the time has come to ensure that what we've built here endures. I want to continue writing a book I started before building the school, not just a collection of recipes but a guide to the principles that define life. A framework for the next generation."

The apprentices exchanged excited glances, their admiration for their mentor evident. One of them, a young chef named Étienne, spoke up with wide-eyed enthusiasm. "Will you teach us, Chef? Will we be part of this?"

Antoine smiled, reflecting on his pride in them. "I'll need your help. This won't be mine alone; it will be ours. Together, we'll show the world that cooking is not just labor but art, science, and philosophy." The room buzzed with energy as the apprentices absorbed the weight of Antoine's words. It was a moment of shared purpose, one that underscored the depth of his influence on those around him.

Voiceover (Older Antoine):

"The decision to write L'Art de la Cuisine Française was not made lightly. I knew it would demand years of meticulous effort, but I also knew it was the most important work of my life. It was more than a book; it was a testament to the lessons I had learned through success and failure, a bridge between the ephemeral beauty of the kitchen and the permanence of the written word."

The months that followed were filled with tireless effort. Antoine's book, *L'Art de la Cuisine Française*, became a labor of love. His writing captured the essence of French haute cuisine: detailed instructions for techniques, sketches of elaborate *pièces montées*, and reflections on the philosophy of cooking. Each page was an offering to future generations, a way to preserve the artistry he had dedicated his life to mastering. Hélène often joined him in the evenings, her presence a steadying force. As Antoine sketched the layers of a vol-au-vent one night, she studied his work with quiet admiration. "You're creating more than a book," she said softly, her voice tinged with pride. "You're building a bridge to the future."

Antoine set down his pen, "It feels like a way to give back, to show my respect, and thank everyone who taught me and supported me. I want others to see what's possible, no matter where they come from."

Hélène leaned over to kiss his cheek. "You've always had a gift for seeing what's possible, Antoine. Now, we'll see it too."

In 1833, after years of painstaking work, *L'Art de la Cuisine Française* was published. Printers worked tirelessly to meet the overwhelming demand, and copies were shipped to culinary schools, courts, and kitchens across Europe. The book was hailed as a masterpiece, a definitive guide to French cuisine that elevated cooking to an intellectual pursuit. The acclaim rejuvenated Antoine. Invitations poured in for him to lecture, demonstrate, and teach. He traveled to Vienna, Berlin, and London, meeting young chefs whose enthusiasm mirrored the spark that had driven him as a boy. Each encounter reaffirmed his belief in the transformative power of the culinary arts.

One particularly notable journey was to the court of Tsar Nicholas I in Russia. The Tsar, aware of Antoine's legacy from his predecessor's reign, invited him to oversee a state banquet. Antoine's pièce montée for the occasion, a sugar palace inspired by St. Petersburg's Winter Palace—was a triumph, its delicate spires and intricate details leaving the gathered dignitaries in awe. "It is more than art," Tsar Nicholas remarked, his voice resonant with admiration. "It is diplomacy on a plate." Antoine listening intently to the Tsar, "Your Majesty, it is an immense honor to serve. I have always believed that food is a language, one that transcends borders and speaks to our shared humanity." The words carried the weight of his journey, a testament to his belief that culinary artistry was not just about taste but about connection.

La Maison de Sucre continued to thrive. Hélène became the soul of the pâtisserie, her warm presence drawing customers who came not just for the desserts but for the sense of belonging the shop offered. Antoine, meanwhile, found joy in mentoring his apprentices, watching as they grew into chefs who carried his vision forward. One evening, as Antoine and Hélène closed the shop together, she turned to him with a quiet smile. "Do you ever think about the boy who sketched towers of sugar in Bailly's bakery?" Antoine chuckled, the memory vivid in his mind. "Every day. He's still here, somewhere. But he's learned to share his dream with others." Hélène leaned her head on his shoulder. "And what a dream it's become." As they stood in the warm glow of the shop, Antoine felt a profound sense of fulfillment. His journey had taken him from the streets of Paris to the grand courts of Europe, yet it was here, in this space made with love and purpose, that he felt truly at home.

Voiceover (Older Antoine):

"Legacy is not about monuments or accolades. It's about the lives we touch, the joy we bring, and the wisdom we leave behind. My work was my voice, but my legacy was in the hands of those who carried it forward."

CHAPTER 24
THE FINAL BANQUET

The crisp autumn air swept through Paris, carrying with it the earthy scent of falling leaves and a sense of quiet introspection. For Antoine Carême, now in the twilight of his life, the season mirrored his own journey—vivid, full of color, but slowly winding toward its inevitable close. Paris was as vibrant as ever, alive with creativity and the murmurings of change, yet for Antoine, the pace of life had shifted. He spent more time reflecting than creating, more time teaching than striving. His legacy carefully fostered over decades, was firmly rooted, but one last chapter remained unwritten.

One evening, as the fading light bathed his apartment overlooking the Seine in a golden glow, a courier arrived with a letter bearing an elaborate crest. Antoine's hands trembled as he broke the seal. It was an invitation from King Louis-Philippe himself, requesting Antoine to arrange a grand banquet at the Palais-Royal. The occasion: a gathering of France's most esteemed thinkers, artists, and diplomats, celebrating France's cultural resurgence.

Antoine ran his fingers over the royal. "One last masterpiece," he murmured, his voice heavy with both resolve and nostalgia. Hélène, seated nearby with a book in her lap, looked up. "You don't have to do this, Antoine," she said gently. "Your name is already written in history. You've done enough." Antoine set the letter down carefully, "It's not about proving anything, Hélène. This is my way of giving back—to the city, to the people, to the craft that gave me a life I never dreamed possible. It's my farewell." Hélène studied him for a moment, then nodded, her smile soft but full of understanding. "Then let's make it unforgettable."

The preparations for the banquet began with an intensity that defied Antoine's years. Though his movements were slower and his body less spry, his mind remained sharp, his vision clear. He gathered his team of apprentices—some now masters in their own right—and unveiled his ambitious plan.

"The menu must be a tapestry of France," he declared, his voice firm but warm. "Every dish should reflect a piece of our heritage. From the earthy stews of the countryside to the refined pastries of Paris, we create a tribute to the soul of our nation."

The pièce montée, the banquet's centerpiece, was to be his final great creation. Antoine envisioned a sculpture that would transcend even his boundaries. A sculpture of Marianne, the embodiment of liberty, draped in flowing ribbons of caramel and surrounded by cascades of marzipan flowers. Fountains of spun sugar would symbolize France's rivers, flowing into delicate pools of chocolate and fruit pastes. It was bold, intricate, and deeply symbolic—a reflection of both the nation's spirit and Antoine's life's work.

"This isn't just a banquet," Antoine told his team during a late-night session in the kitchen. "It's a story. Each element must speak, not just to the palate but to the entirety of a person."

The apprentices, inspired by his passion, poured their own hearts into the work. Hélène, ever by his side, managed the logistics, ensuring every detail was perfect. Though Antoine's sometimes faltered, his will never waver.

On the evening of the banquet, the Palais-Royal was transformed into a scene of breathtaking elegance. The grand hall sparkled with candlelight, its high ceilings adorned with garlands of flowers and silk draperies. Guests arrived in their finest attire, their anticipation palpable. They were not just here to celebrate France; they were here to witness the final masterpiece of its greatest chef.

As the courses began to flow from the kitchen, a hush fell over the room. Each dish was a testament to Antoine's vision: delicate consommés that shimmered like liquid gold, roasts seasoned with herbs that evoked the French countryside, and pastries so intricate they seemed almost too beautiful to eat.

When the pièce montée was unveiled, gasps echoed through the hall. The sugar sculpture of Marianne stood illuminated at the room's center, her features serene yet strong, surrounded by cascading marzipan roses and shimmering sugar streams. The craftsmanship was flawless, the symbolism profound.

King Louis-Philippe rose from his seat, his voice cutting through the silence. "Monsieur Carême," he declared, his tone rich with admiration, "you have given us more than a feast. You have given us a vision of France's soul. For this, we are forever in your debt." The applause that followed washed over him like a warm embrace. For a moment, he allowed himself to soak in the culmination of a lifetime's work.

Voiceover (Older Antoine):

"That night at the Palais-Royal was more than a banquet. It was a reflection of everything I had lived for. As I stood in that room, surrounded by the beauty of creation and the warmth of gratitude, I understood that my work had never been about me. It had always been about them—the people, the stories, the connections. And in that understanding, I found peace."

In the weeks that followed, Antoine began to step back from the bustling kitchen of *La Maison de Sucre*. He entrusted its care to his apprentices, confident in their ability to carry forward his vision. His days became quieter, filled with long walks through Paris, market visits, and hours spent sketching in his notebooks.

One afternoon, as he and Hélène sat by the Seine, Antoine turned to her with a thoughtful expression. "I've been thinking," he said. "I want to write one more book, not about recipes or techniques, but about the cooking philosophy. About why we do what we do."

Hélène's smile was warm and encouraging. "I believe you should." The idea sparked a quiet excitement within him. "It won't be for the chefs. It will be for everyone, anyone who has ever found joy in a meal, a moment, a connection."

The Final Days

As winter descended on Paris, Antoine's health began to decline at an alarming rate. Yet, he remained content, always filled with the knowledge that he had given everything to his craft and the people he loved. Surrounded by Hélène, his apprentices, and friends, he spent his final days in quiet reflection, the fire of his existence giving way to a serene glow of fulfillment.

On a crisp morning in January, as the first light of dawn touched the rooftops of Paris, Antoine Carême passed away peacefully. His death was met with an outpouring of grief from the city he had loved and inspired. Paris mourned its greatest chef, but his spirit endured in every kitchen, every pâtisserie, every creation inspired by his life's work.

Voiceover (Older Antoine):

"My journey was never about reaching a destination. It was about the steps, the moments, the people. Each creation was a story, each banquet a chapter. As I leave this earth, I do so with the knowledge that my passion and love for creations will be illuminating the paths of those who will follow."

CHAPTER 25
A NEW GENERATION

*L*a Maison de Sucre became a symbol of Antoine's enduring influence, its doors welcoming visitors from all over. Chefs who had studied under him carried his techniques and philosophy to new lands, spreading the gospel of French cuisine. In kitchens, books, and minds, the legacy of Antoine Carême lived on. He had not just changed what we see as food; he had elevated it, showing that creation was an act of love and that love could change empires. *La Maison de Sucre* stood as both a physical monument and a living tribute to his artistry. Situated in the heart of Paris, it had become more than a pâtisserie; it was a pilgrimage site for dreamers, chefs, artists, and travelers. To step inside was to enter a domain where sugar became sculpture, flour turned to poetry, and food rose beyond its earthly origins, becoming a reflection of the divine. The walls echoed with whispered stories of kings served and courts amazed, of struggles overcome, and beauty forged. Beneath its gleaming windows and ornate arches, Antoine Carême's spirit, not as a shadow but as a light, illuminating the path for those who followed.

Hélène: The Keeper of Dreams

Time had left its mark on Hélène, but it had not dimmed her spirit. Though her hair had silvered, and her hands bore the delicate traces of age, she moved through the bustling kitchen of La Maison de Sucre with the same quiet authority she always had. She was no longer just an advisor or a friend; she was the last living thread to Antoine's legacy, the keeper of his dreams. To Hélène, this place was more than a school, more than a shop. It was sacred ground. Every delicate pastry that emerged from its ovens, sugar sculpture that gleamed under the display lights and a whisper of flour and butter in the air carried his name.

She paused beside a group of apprentices, their brows crinkly in concentration as they carefully layered the pâte feuilletée for mille-feuille. Their hands trembled slightly, cautious but eager, as they pressed and folded the dough. "Do not rush," Hélène said gently, her voice carrying the wisdom of years. "Patience is as much an ingredient as sugar or butter. Each layer must rise and crisp as though kissed by the air itself."

One of the apprentices, a boy no older than Antoine had been when he first stepped into a kitchen, glanced up with a nervous smile. "Yes, Madame Hélène. We'll get it right." She returned the smile with an encouraging gesture before continuing her walk through the kitchen. She knew these young chefs were more than students; they were inheritors of a dream that had outlived the man who built it. At last, she stopped in a quiet corner, where a glass display case held one of Antoine's final sketches—unfinished yet brimming with life. It was meant to be a grand sugar masterpiece, a rendering of the Seine itself, with spun sugar waves flowing beneath delicate caramel bridges, boats drifting along its crystalline current, each ripple carefully etched.

Hélène reached out, her fingertips tracing the edge of the glass as if trying to touch the dream he had left behind. Her voice, soft but unwavering, barely rose above a whisper. "You never stopped dreaming, Antoine. Not for a single moment." And neither would she.

The Reach of L'Art de la Cuisine Française

Antoine's *L'Art de la Cuisine Française* had grown into far more than a book; it had become the cornerstone of culinary education. Across Europe and beyond, chefs studied its pages with reverence. It was not just a compilation of recipes but a manifesto of artistry and purpose. The book celebrated Antoine's breakthroughs: tempered sugar's structural integrity, pastry layering architecture, and techniques for spinning sugar into lace-like threads of fragile beauty. In his philosophy, food was art and science in perfect balance, something that delighted the visual senses before pleasing the palate.

In Vienna, a bakery adorned its windows with towering sugar creations modeled after Antoine's pièces montées. In St. Petersburg, chefs studied his methods to honor dignitaries with confections that seemed to dance in candlelight. In London, culinary schools added Antoine's name to their halls of fame, his legacy firmly etched into gastronomy. Yet it was more than a technique that spread. His words carried forward his ideals that food could be art, that beauty was a form of love, and that a simple dish could unite the hearts of those who shared it.

The fiftieth anniversary of *La Maison de Sucre* marked a momentous occasion. It was an evening where time seemed to fold upon itself, past and present intertwined. The kitchen buzzed with anticipation as master chefs, once Antoine's apprentices, crafted the pièce montée in memory of their mentor. The banquet hall was filled with luminaries from across Europe: chefs, artists, philosophers, and patrons who had long admired Antoine's work. The room was bathed in golden light and a quiet awe when the final creation was unveiled. The pièce montée towered like a cathedral of dreams—A sugar replica of Notre Dame, just like the one Antoine had designed for the grand opening of La Maison de Sucre 50 years ago surrounded by delicate symbols of cities Antoine had touched. Vienna's opera house, St. Petersburg's palaces, and London's iconic bridges stood at its base, woven together by spun sugar ribbons that flowed like rivers. It was a masterpiece not only of skill but of storytelling, a tribute to a life that had reshaped food. Applause thundered through the hall, yet at the edge of the room, Hélène stood quietly, her hand resting over her heart. She could almost hear Antoine's voice, as clear as if he were beside her. "Legacy isn't formed in monuments or accolades," he had once said. "It's in the lives we touch, the joy we create, and the dreams we inspire."

As change continued, *La Maison de Sucre* adapted to it but never lost its soul. The next generation of chefs carried forward Antoine's vision, infusing it with their own creativity. Young artisans experimented with new flavors and techniques, blending tradition with innovation in ways Antoine himself would have admired. On the morning after the gala, as the first light broke over Paris, Hélène stood on the bakery's balcony, gazing at the people. In her hands was a delicate macaron—simple, perfect, a small miracle of texture and taste. She bit into it slowly, savoring the crisp shell and the burst of filling. For a moment, it was as if time had stilled. "To you, Antoine," she whispered, her voice carried delicately by the wind. "To the fire you lit—and to those who keep it."

The Eternal Flow

Paris continued with life; the Seine flowed on—timeless and steady. It carried with it the story of a boy who had once sketched sugar towers in an unpretentious bakery, a man who had redefined what was possible with flour and sugar. Antoine Carême lived not only in the kitchens of Europe but in those dreamers and believers of beautiful things. In the quiet corners of *La Maison de Sucre*, children still pressed their faces to the glass, full of wonder at sugar castles and caramel fountains. Young chefs worked through the night perfecting their technique, whispering words of encouragement to one another as they perfected Antoine's techniques. And somewhere in the laughter, the applause, and the quiet moments of creation, the fire he ignited burned on—eternal, unyielding, and sweet.

Voiceover (Hélène):

"Antoine once told me that creation is the closest we come to eternity. Each piece of art, each morsel of beauty, is a bridge between the fleeting and the infinite. And so, he lives on—not just in sugar and flour, but in every dream inspired by his vigor."

As the city of Paris slept under a silver moon, *La Maison de Sucre* stood like a beacon, its windows glowing with warmth. Antoine's kingdom, built not of stone but of sugar and dreams, remained eternal.

CHAPTER 26
THE FLAMES LIVE ON

Paris had changed. The decades had brought new marvels to the city, the wrought iron lace of the Eiffel Tower now dominated the skyline, the rhythm of life faster, the pulse of industry steady and unrelenting. Yet, amidst this modern age, La Maison de Sucre stood as an enduring symbol, its gilded facade unbowed by time. An ideal of beauty. A place where Antoine Carême's fire still burned. For generations, the pâtisserie had passed from skilled hands to visionaries, each caretaker honoring its past while daring to imagine its future. Now, it belonged to Juliette, the granddaughter of one of Antoine's earliest apprentices and a woman who carried the weight of the past with both pride and quiet apprehension.

The morning light streamed through the tall, elegant windows of La Maison de Sucre, illuminating the bustling kitchen. The air was alive with the mingling scents of vanilla, caramelized sugar, rising pastry, and an aura of purpose. Juliette moved like a conductor among her team, young apprentices whose eager faces reflected the spark of creativity she remembered from her own childhood. Her voice carried gently over the kitchen noise, guiding with both exactitude and warmth. "Steady hands, Léon. The sugar must shine like glass, not dull like sand." "Yes, Chef," came the earnest reply as the young apprentice corrected his movements. On the counter before her lay her newest design: a pièce montée inspired by modern Paris. It was a bold step, one that sought to capture the city's evolving spirit while paying homage to its past. A sugar Eiffel Tower rose as the centerpiece, delicate yet imposing, surrounded by spun sugar bridges and marzipan façades of the Louvre. At the base, a ribbon of blue spun sugar mimicked the Seine, its sparkling surface a tribute to the eternal river. "This is our chance to tell a story," Juliette said, addressing the team as they gathered to admire the sketches. "Antoine Carême taught us that beauty exists in both structure and soul. He constantly pushed boundaries in all his endeavors. Today, we honor him by embracing his spirit of innovation." The weight of her words inspires a flurry of renewed focus.

That evening, after the last pastries had been boxed and the kitchens fell silent, Juliette wandered through the quiet pâtisserie. The glass cases, now empty, reflected the flickering light of the chandeliers above. She made her way to the far corner of the shop where Antoine's final, unfinished sketch rested beneath the glass, a sugar rendering of the Seine, its flowing beauty captured in delicate arcs and spun sugar ribbons. Juliette traced the edge of the case with her fingertips, the same way Antoine would do, her voice barely a whisper. "Did you know how far this would reach, Antoine?" Her thoughts drifted to the stories she had grown up with: how Antoine had sketched sugar palaces under flickering lamplight, how he had redefined cuisine as an art form, how he had given everything to that life, leaving behind a legacy as delicate and enduring as the sugar sculptures he had shaped.

Voiceover (Juliette):

"Antoine Carême's legacy is more than recipes, techniques, or precision. It's courage. The courage to dream, create, and believe that even a fleeting creation can touch eternity. That is what he left us."

The unveiling of the pièce montée arrived like an electric charge for the city. Word had spread of the audacious design, a sugar homage to Paris itself and the pâtisserie moved with passion and intensity in preparation for the event. When the time came, the grand salon of La Maison de Sucre was filled with dignitaries, artists, and admirers from across the city. The pièce montée stood at the center, illuminated by golden light: a modern tribute to Antoine's spirit, towering yet graceful, a bridge between the old and the new.

As the final cloth was pulled away, the room fell into awed silence. Gasps rippled through the crowd as the full splendor of the pièce montée was revealed. Before them stood Paris in sugar—a delicate spun-sugar lattice forming the Eiffel Tower, its intricate lines catching the candlelight; the marzipan reflections of the Louvre's grand facade, so precise it seemed almost to breathe; and the shimmering river of caramel and isomalt, flowing endlessly around its base, as if the Seine itself had been frozen in time.

The creation was more than a display of skill. It was alive—a testament to time, resilience, and the unbreakable spirit of creation. Amid the murmurs of admiration, an older man stepped forward. His face was deeply lined, his shoulders slightly stooped with age, but his gaze was sharp, filled with recognition, warmth, and memory.

Juliette turned as he approached, sensing before he spoke that he had known Antoine and had stood in the kitchens where history had been shaped. He studied the sugar sculpture in silence before finally speaking, his voice gravelly yet rich with pride.

"You've honored him well."

Juliette smiled, feeling the weight of history in his words. "We stand on his shoulders. And yours." The old man chuckled softly, his eyes lingering on the sugar-crafted city. "Ah, but you have given it your own voice. That is what he would have wanted. The flame is passed, but it never dims."

Long after the guests had departed, long after the last glass of champagne had been drained and the lights had dimmed, Juliette found herself alone in the kitchen. The silence was comforting, filled with the echoes of the evening's triumph. As she moved to tidy a back shelf, her fingers brushed against something unexpected: a small, forgotten notebook tucked behind a row of jars. The leather was soft, worn with time, and its spine cracked from years of use. She pulled it free, her heartbeat quickening. The moment she opened it, she knew. The handwriting, elegant, deliberate, was his. Antoine's.

Her breath caught as she read the words inscribed on the first page, penned in ink that had faded but never lost its weight:

"To those who carry this forward: Remember, every creation is a story. Make yours unforgettable."

Tears welled in her eyes as she ran her fingers over the words. It was as though Antoine himself had spoken to her across time, his message clear, unwavering. She closed the notebook gently, holding it to her chest. The legacy was alive. And it was hers to carry forward.

Voiceover (Older Juliette):

"La Maison de Sucre is more than a pâtisserie. It's a promise—a promise that creation, no matter how fleeting, can leave an everlasting mark. It is a reminder that greatness lies in the courage to imagine, risk, and give a part of yourself."

Juliette carried the notebook to her desk, placing it carefully alongside her own designs. She sat for a moment, surrounded by the tranquil ambiance of the pâtisserie. She could feel Antoine's presence, not as a shadow, but as a light, guiding her forward. She rose and walked to the window, looking out over the twinkling lights of Paris. The city stretched before her, vast and eternal, the same city Antoine had once loved so deeply. "To you, Chef," she whispered, raising an invisible toast to the night. "And to the dreams yet to come." Below, the kitchens ignited with life once more, the steady sounds of soft laughter echoing through the walls. The next generation was already at work, shaping sugar and flour into their own stories, carried forward, never fading.

Final Voiceover (Juliette):

"The flame Antoine Carême will never be extinguished, not just in La Maison de Sucre, but in all kitchens in every romantic, every chef who believes that food is more than sustenance, and every artist who sees beauty where others see the ordinary. His story, our story, will never end."

As the city slept, La Maison de Sucre remained radiant, its light a symbol of Antoine's eternal legacy, a flame passed down through generations. For as long as there were dreamers, the fire would live on.

CHAPTER 27
THE CIRCLE COMPLETES

Decades had turned like the pages of an old book, and Paris continued its eternal transformation. The skyline was now a mosaic of history and modernity, with soaring iron towers and stone cathedrals standing side by side. Amidst the city's evolution, La Maison de Sucre remained an unchanging sanctuary where art, tradition, and dreams converged. For the city's people, the pâtisserie had become more than a culinary institution; it was a pilgrimage site, a testament to what was possible. Antoine Carême's name lived on in whispered reverence.

Juliette, now in her sixties but still commanding the quiet power of a master at work, stood at the entrance of La Maison de Sucre one crisp morning, observing the bustling streets of Paris, where vendors called out, and carriages rattled over cobblestones. Life moved quickly now, yet the pâtisserie remained timeless with its elegant facade and warm glow.

This year marked the centennial anniversary of La Maison de Sucre, a milestone that carried the weight of memory and the promise of future dreams. To commemorate the occasion, Juliette had planned something extraordinary: a global symposium of chefs and culinary historians, all gathering to remember Antoine Carême, the man who had reshaped our understanding of cuisine.

Inside the kitchen, Juliette's team worked with focused energy, their hands steady, their movements purposeful. Every flick of the wrist, every delicate placement of sugar, was infused with precision and reverence. At the heart of their preparations stood the pièce montée that would define the evening, a breathtaking sugar sculpture unlike any before it. Instead of the Eiffel Tower or a grand palace, they had crafted a sugar astrolabe, its golden rings entwined in delicate caramel filigree, the markings of constellations and celestial paths glistening under the kitchen's warm glow. It was not just a tribute to Antoine's artistry but to his vision, the way he mapped the future of pastry, and the way his influence had spread like the stars across continents.

Encircling the base were sugar renditions of the tools of his trade, a meticulously sculpted rolling pin, a delicate copper saucepan, and a bound sugar replica of L'Art de la Cuisine Française, its pages seeming almost to turn with the lightest breath. Interwoven between them were sugar banners, each inscribed with a different name: Paris, St. Petersburg, Vienna, London, Bavaria, each place where Antoine had left his mark. Juliette took a step back, studying the creation. This was more than a homage; it was a testament to how far his legacy had traveled and how much further it would go. She turned to her team; their faces lit with the same quiet determination that had fueled Antoine's own ambitions so many years ago. "Remember," she said, "we are not just honoring Antoine's past. We are honoring the future he dreamed of, the one we are building now. Each detail must carry the same care he gave to his work. His legacy is not something we inherit; it is something we continue." A calm resolve passed through the room, a silent understanding that this was more than just sugar, nougatine, and craftsmanship. It was a calling.

On the evening of the symposium, La Maison de Sucre sparkled beneath strings of lights, its grand salon transformed into a gathering place for the world's greatest culinary minds. Chefs had traveled from Kyoto, Buenos Aires, London, and Moscow, each carrying their own stories and influences but all bound by the common thread of Antoine's legacy. Many held copies of his L'Art de la Cuisine Française, its pages worn, some smudged with flour and sugar from years of study. His influence had become a bridge, not just between nations, but between generations. When the pièce montée was unveiled, the room fell into an enchanted silence.

The sugar astrolabe shimmered under the candlelight, its caramel constellations casting delicate shadows as if the heavens themselves had been charted in sugar. The tools of Antoine's craft stood proud at its base, symbols of the empire he had built not through power but through artistry. The crowd did not erupt into applause immediately. Instead, for a moment, there was only awe, the kind of reverence reserved for something truly timeless. Then, slowly at first and rising like a wave, the applause and cheers filled the room. Juliette stepped forward, her heart full. Though age had softened her voice, it still carried the warmth and authority of someone who had spent a lifetime devoted to her craft. "Tonight, we stand on the shoulders of a dreamer," she began. "Antoine Carême taught us that food is more than sustenance; it is a bridge between people, cultures, and generations. His vision reshaped our craft, but more importantly, it reminded us of the power of creation. Each of you carries that fire, and that is his true legacy."

The applause this time was thunderous, not just for what had been made but for what it represented.

Later that evening, as the celebration wound down, Juliette found herself speaking with a young pastry chef named Émile. He was barely twenty, his pristine chef's coat still crisp from the night's excitement, his hands gripping a copy of L'Art de la Cuisine Française as though it were a sacred text. His voice trembled slightly as he spoke. "Madame Juliette... I came from Lyon just for this. Your work and Antoine's legacy have been my guide. I've spent years trying to master his sugar techniques. Someday, I hope to create something that inspires others the way he has inspired me." Juliette smiled, feeling a familiar warmth stir within her. "Then you already understand the most important lesson," she said, resting a gentle hand on the worn book. "Antoine's gift was never just about the sugar, the pastry, or the spectacle. It was about telling a story. Keep learning. Keep creating. And when the time comes, make sure your story is worth telling." Émile's eyes shone with quiet determination, and in that moment, Juliette saw the future—not just of what Antoine left behind, but of the world he had helped shape. The flame had been passed. And it would never dim.

Juliette's smile was kind, her spirit swelling at the earnestness in his voice. "You already have something Antoine valued most," she said, placing a gentle hand on his shoulder. "The courage to dream. Hold onto that, Émile. Every creation you make is a chance to tell your story. Make it one worth remembering." The young chef glistened with emotion. "I will, Madame. I promise."

Voiceover (Juliette):

"Legacy is not a monument frozen in time. It grows, evolves, and weaves itself into those it touches, not just in the kitchens of La Maison de Sucre. This is where dreamers like Émile continue to shape the future."

As the evening ended, Juliette slipped away to the balcony. The river stretched out below her, its waters flowing endlessly, reflecting the lights of Paris in its ripples. For a moment, she imagined Antoine standing here, looking out at this same city, alive with his dreams and possibilities. She raised her glass to the stars. "To you, Antoine. And to the dreamers yet to come." Behind her, the kitchen of La Maison de Sucre, the sound of whisks against metal, the crackle of caramelizing sugar, the quiet laughter of young chefs, a symphony of creation that carried Antoine's spirit forward.

Final Voiceover (Juliette):

"The art of creation is the art of connection. To our past, each other, and the dreams we leave for those who follow. Antoine Carême's story will never end because he lives in every sugar ribbon spun and every soul brave enough to imagine beauty where others see the ordinary."

As midnight fell, La Maison de Sucre stood like a lighthouse in the heart of Paris, its windows aglow with warmth and light. Inside, Émile and the other apprentices worked into the quiet hours, their hands crafting pastries and sculptures under a portrait of Antoine hanging on the wall. In this place, past and future danced together, a reminder that true artistry is eternal, passed on through generations like an unquenchable flame. And so, the circle completed itself, carrying forward the legacy of a boy who had dreamed in sugar and flour and a man who had reshaped his art.

CHAPTER 28
THE ETERNAL TABLE

The early morning sun spilled across the rooftops of Paris, bathing the city in golden hues. The surface of the Seine glistened like a ribbon of light, winding through the city that seemed timeless yet ever-changing. At its center stood La Maison de Sucre, its ornate facade glowing softly in the dawn. The pâtisserie had stood for a century, its doors welcoming dreamers, artists, and beauty lovers.

This day, however, was different. Today, Paris and all culinarians celebrated the centennial anniversary of Antoine Carême's death. Once again, the event had drawn chefs, historians, dignitaries, and admirers from every corner of the globe. It was not just a celebration of the man himself but a tribute to the art of creation, to the belief that food could be more than sustenance—it could be a language, a bridge, and a legacy.

Juliette stood in the main kitchen of La Maison de Sucre, surrounded by her team. At eighty, she had become a matriarch in her own right, the threads of Antoine's vision woven into her very being. Her silver hair was tied back neatly, her chef's coat pristine. She moved through the kitchen with a quiet authority, filled with both pride and reverence as her team worked tirelessly. "Every detail matters, as you all know, but especially today," Juliette said, her voice carrying above the sound of the kitchen and the sizzle of caramelizing sugar. "This is not just about Antoine's memory. It's about what he gave us and the passion we now give."

The pièce montée that would crown the celebration stood at the center of the kitchen, unfinished but already breathtaking. It was a sugar tree of life, its branches sprawling outward like delicate lacework. Each branch held symbols of Antoine's influence: a spinning globe rendered in sugar, towers inspired by his grand architectural pièces montées, and small sugar figures of chefs at work, an homage to every generation he has touched. At its base was the centerpiece: a sculpted figure of Antoine Carême himself, kneeling beside his first oven, the tools of his trade in hand, as if looking toward the future he had inspired. Juliette paused, staring at the sculpture with tears reflecting the light. "He would have loved this," she whispered.

Voiceover (Juliette):

"Antoine always saw beyond what others could see. He dreamed of beauty when there was none, and he found possibility in the simplest of ingredients. This tree, this day, it is our way of saying 'thank you.' Not for what he made, but for what he taught us to believe in." The morning light gave way to a dazzling afternoon as guests arrived at La Maison de Sucre. The air buzzed with excitement as chefs in immaculate coats, historians clutching well-worn copies of *L'Art de la Cuisine Française*, and families carrying small children passed through the pâtisserie's doors.

The grand salon had been transformed into a gallery of Antoine's life and work. Tables were adorned with smaller sugar sculptures inspired by his designs, a carousel of delicate swans, a lace-like cathedral, a towering pagoda, and walls were lined with sketches, photographs, and letters chronicling his journey. Juliette walked through the crowd, taking in the faces of those who had come to pay tribute. She paused to listen to conversations:

"He was the father of modern cuisine."

"Did you see the sugar work on that tower? Incredible."

"His book changed my life as a chef."

Among the crowd was a small group of students from a Parisian culinary academy. Their instructor, an older chef, gestured toward a sketch of Antoine's sugar palace and said, "Look closely. Carême didn't just make food—he told stories. Your job is not just to cook but to dream." The students stared at the sketch with awe, their young faces reflecting the same wonder that had once driven Antoine to imagine sugar cathedrals in a baker's cellar.

When the pièce montée was finally unveiled, the room fell into a hushed reverence. The sugar tree seemed to shimmer under the light of the grand chandelier, its branches arching gracefully upward as though reaching toward the heavens. At its base, the figure of Antoine looked small yet powerful, his presence a reminder of where it all began. Juliette stepped forward to address the crowd, her voice full of emotion. "Antoine Carême taught us that art is not limited to canvas or stone," she began. "It can be found in the humblest of kitchens, in the flour on our hands, in the sugar spun into lace. He saw beauty where others saw only necessity. not for himself, but for all of us." She paused, her eyes sweeping the room. "This tree is a symbol of that dream. Its roots stretch into the past, nourished by what he left us, and its branches extend into the future, held up by all of you. This is his table, and you are all seated at it." The ovation that followed was thunderous, echoing through the walls of La Maison de Sucre like a symphony.

As the evening wore on, Juliette wandered through the grand kitchen, her fingers grazing the worn wooden worktables where generations of chefs had toiled. The air still carried the faint aroma of caramelized sugar and warm pastry, mingling with the celebratory hum beyond the doors. She paused before an old copper mold, its surface gleaming under the soft glow of candlelight. With careful hands, she lifted it, running her thumb over the engraved initials, Antoine's mark, a testament to his craft. A quiet smile played on her lips as she set it down, then reached for a pristine linen cloth. Slowly, methodically, she polished the mold as if preserving a fragment of his legacy. "To Antoine," she murmured, the whisper dissolving into the night. "To the hands that shaped the future."

Voiceover (Juliette):

"Some lives are like candles, their flames small but steady. But others—like Antoine's—burn brighter, lighting paths for generations to follow. His legacy is not just in the sugar palaces or the recipes he left behind, but in every chef, every dreamer, every hand that turns flour and sugar into art."

As midnight approached, the last guests trickled from La Maison de Sucre, their voices carrying the weight of a shared wonder. Inside, the kitchen still hummed with life. Young apprentices worked by the glow of lamps, their hands steady as they piped cream and tempered sugar, their faces lit by the same ardor that had filled Antoine so long ago. On the wall, Antoine Carême's portrait watched over them; his portrait always seemed to be gazing down at all of them in a protective and hopeful manner, his expression filled with possibility.

La Maison de Sucre stood as it always had, a tower of brilliance and vision, its windows agleam against the dark. The sugar tree, bathed in the soft light of the chandeliers, seemed to whisper its stories to the empty salon. The circle had completed itself, yet it remained unbroken, stretching onward, carried by those who believed in the power of creation. Antoine Carême's spirit was eternal as the city that had raised him, the hands that carried him, and the steps that made him who he had become.

CHAPTER 29
A TIMELESS VISION

A s the years continued their steady march, Antoine Carême's name became more than a symbol of culinary excellence; it became a touchstone for the universal power of creation. The world had changed, its borders and boundaries redrawn by history, yet his influence endured. From the patisseries of Paris to distant kitchens in Tokyo and New York, his vision resonated with those who believed food could transcend sustenance to become something far greater: a story, a bridge, a legacy.

At the core of this transformation stood Juliette, custodian of La Maison de Sucre, whose determination had breathed new life into Antoine's dream. Now in her nineties, her presence carried a quiet authority, a confidence tempered by the challenges of leadership but fueled by an unshakable belief in the pâtisserie's mission. Under her care, La Maison de Sucre was no longer just a patisserie; it had evolved into a learning hub, a place where Antoine's vision expanded into uncharted territories.

On a crisp spring morning, Juliette, much older now but still strong, addressed a class of aspiring pastry chefs in the newly completed Culinary Atelier, a state-of-the-art teaching kitchen. The walls bore framed pages of Antoine's original sketches, juxtaposed with photographs of young chefs from across the globe, their work inspired by his techniques. "Antoine Carême didn't just bake," Juliette began, her voice firm yet warm. "He imagined. He believed that food was art and that art could touch the human soul. He didn't stop at what was possible; he reached for what could be. That's why you're here, not just to learn, but to dream." The students sat enthralled, their eyes radiating with a mix of awe and hope. Among them was Isabelle, a timid but talented young chef from Buenos Aires who had won a scholarship to study at the atelier. Her hands shook a little as she took notes, overwhelmed by the magnitude of where she was.

Juliette approached Isabelle's station later that day, her tone gentle. "Your hands may shake, but I can already see your strength in what you create. Trust yourself." Isabelle's expression shifted to one of quiet strength. "I will, Madame Juliette. I promise." Juliette's stewardship of La Maison de Sucre extended far beyond Paris. Over the years, she had cultivated relationships with chefs, bakers, and culinary schools across continents, ensuring Antoine's techniques reached those who sought to embrace tradition while daring to innovate.

One such connection was in Kyoto, Japan, where Chef Haruto, a master of wagashi, the delicate art of Japanese confections, had integrated Antoine's sugar-spinning techniques into his own creations. His most famous piece, a sugar cherry blossom suspended within a spun sugar dome, had become a celebrated link between French and Japanese Culinary artists. In a letter to Juliette, Haruto wrote:

"Antoine Carême taught me that boundaries are an illusion. In my sugar, I find his spirit. In his techniques, I hear my ancestor's whisper. This is how creation unites us across oceans and time."

Juliette kept these letters—dozens of them—in a small, leather-bound book in her office. Each one was a testament to Antoine's enduring influence, from the bustling bakeries of Mumbai to the haute patisseries of New York. Late one evening, Juliette found herself in the archives of La Maison de Sucre, combing through documents she had carefully preserved over the years. Her fingers brushed against a small, timeworn journal tucked behind Antoine's original sketches. It was his handwriting, elegant, precise, and it seemed almost as if he were speaking to her through the pages.

One passage caught her breath:

"To create is to leave a piece of yourself behind. Not for praise or wealth, but for connection—to touch someone who may never know your name."

Juliette sat in the quiet, tears brimming up as she absorbed the weight of his words. For years, she had carried the torch of Antoine's dream, but this moment reminded her why. It was not for glory or recognition but for the lives they touched and the bridges they built. "I'll make sure you're never forgotten," she whispered into the stillness, a promise not to Antoine but to herself.

The following day, Juliette's team gathered in the grand kitchen, preparing to construct a *pièce montée* for an international gala honoring the evolution of culinary artistry. The design was ambitious, an homage to Antoine's legacy, yet boldly innovative. At its center stood a towering spire of spun caramel, reaching skyward like the spires of Notre Dame, delicate yet commanding, each golden thread capturing the essence of ambition and craftsmanship. The kitchen pulsed with controlled urgency, the team working in harmony, each movement a note in a well-rehearsed symphony. Among them, Émile observed, his eyes tracing the rise of the structure as it took form. It was unlike anything *La Maison de Sucre* had attempted before—a challenge that tested skill, patience, and vision.

In the quieter corner of the kitchen, Isabelle worked on a separate piece, her hands steady as she carefully assembled a miniature rendition of Antoine's famed *Grecian temple*. It was not part of the main display but something she had crafted on her own, driven by admiration and an unspoken desire to leave her own mark. The columns leaned slightly, the sugarwork not as refined as Antoine's, yet there was something in it, an honesty, a passion, that made it beautiful. Juliette approached, studying the piece with careful eyes before lifting it gently. A slow smile curved her lips. "This is your voice, Isabelle," she said, running a thumb over the fine details. "Perfection isn't always the goal. It's the truth of the creation that matters most." Isabelle's face lit with pride and understanding. "Thank you, Madame Juliette. I see it now."

Émile listened from a distance, his gaze shifting back to the rising spire of caramel, its golden glow catching the light. He had spent years chasing the past, measuring himself against legends. But standing here, in the hum of creation, he realized something vital: legacy wasn't about replication. It was about evolution. The past had built the foundation. But today, they were reaching for something greater—something entirely their own.

Voiceover (Juliette): *"A legacy is not defined by what we leave behind, but by how we inspire others to carry it forward. Antoine Carême showed us that creation can outlive time itself, whether in sugar, flour, or dreams. And as long as there are those who believe in creating magnificence, his ideas will never fade."*

La Maison de Sucre stands proudly against the Parisian skyline, its windows aflame with the light of new beginnings. Inside, young chefs gather around their workstations, their hands shaping creations that carry whispers of the past and the hope of the future. From Kyoto to Buenos Aires, Paris to New York, the generational inspiration Antoine Carême had ignited continues to spread, lighting hearts, connecting souls, and proving that the art of creation is, indeed, eternal.

PART VI
THE GLOBAL TABLE

CHAPTER 30
A NEW DAWN

Paris was shrouded in a soft mist as the first golden rays of dawn touched the Seine. The river glimmered in hues of pink and gold, its gentle flow a timeless rhythm that had watched over the city for centuries. Even as the world shifted around it, the river remained constant, much like *La Maison de Sucre*, a sanctuary of artistry and ambition that stood resolute through the changing tides of time.

Inside its storied walls, the pâtisserie stirred to life. The faint crackle of ovens heating, the soft thud of dough meeting marble, and the sweet, heady aroma of sugar and cream wove together, a symphony of tradition and renewal. It was a scene that had played out for over a hundred years, but today, it carried an even deeper resonance.

Juliette was gone, in presence but never in spirit. Her touch remained in the meticulous folds of laminated dough, in the delicate balance of flavors perfected over generations, in the very walls that had absorbed her laughter and quiet dedication. Though she had stepped away, her continuation of what Antoine left had endured, not as a shadow of the past but as a guiding light for the future. And the future had a name.

Émile stood in the center of the kitchen, the soft morning light catching in his flour-dusted hair. He rolled his sleeves higher, revealing arms strong from years of practice, hands steady with purpose. He was not Juliette, nor did he seek to be. He was something new, a conduit between past and present, between tradition and reinvention.

Today, *La Maison de Sucre* was his to shepherd. Not alone, but with the wisdom of those who had come before him and the boundless potential of those yet to follow. Émile surveyed the kitchen with pride as his team, a blend of veterans and eager apprentices, prepared for the day. Today marked the fiftieth anniversary of Juliette's stewardship of La Maison de Sucre, and Émile intended to honor her by unveiling a creation that reflected both their legacy and their future. "Let's remember what this place stands for," Émile said, addressing the team. "Each pastry, each piece of sugar, carries a story. Our story, Antoine's story. Let's make something worthy of the generations who brought us here and the ones who will carry us forward."

Among the team was Clara, a brilliant but headstrong young chef who had joined *La Maison de Sucre* two years ago. Her talent was undeniable, but her ambition often outpaced her patience. As she worked, rolling out delicate sheets of *pâte sucrée*, Émile noticed the tension in her movements, the urgency that threatened to undo the precision the dough required. He paused by her station, watching for a moment before speaking.

"Slow down, Clara," he said gently. "The secret isn't speed; it's care." She looked up, her face flushed with frustration. "But Chef, we'll fall behind." Émile gave a faint smile, shaking his head. "No masterpiece was ever made in haste. Beauty takes time." The words lingered between them, but Émile felt their weight settle deeper within himself. He had heard the stories, tales of Antoine's relentless pursuit of perfection, nights spent salvaging delicate confections ruined by envious hands, and obstacles met not with anger but with quiet, unwavering determination. Antoine had rebuilt, refined, and triumphed, not just through skill but through resilience. He needed Clara to focus on the task before her, not get lost in the legends of Antoine. Émile could almost hear Juliette's voice recounting those moments, the reverence in her tone, the quiet admiration. But those stories would wait. Today was not about the past; it was about proving, through his own hands, that he belonged in this lineage of dedication and artistry, as well as guiding the next generation of culinary artisans. Clara exhaled slowly, her fingers relaxing on the rolling pin. The frustration that had tightened her movements softened, replaced by focus. Émile's words settled into her like a seed, not yet bloomed but ready to take root.

Later that morning, Émile stepped into the archives that Juliette had carefully preserved. The small, windowless room had grown into a living library of Antoine's legacy: notebooks filled with sketches, letters from chefs across the globe, and framed photographs of past generations, Juliette among them, her smile radiant as she stood at the helm of La Maison de Sucre. Émile, with a feeling of connection, ran his fingers over one of Antoine's original journals, its leather worn smooth by time and reverence. A particular entry caught his eye:

"Our work does not belong to us. It belongs to those who come after us, who dare to dream beyond our reach."

He exhaled deeply, the words anchoring him in the present. Antoine had set the table, Juliette had carried the torch, and now it was his turn to ensure the flame continued to burn.

To mark the anniversary, Émile had organized a special gala at La Maison de Sucre, one that brought together chefs, culinary historians, and students from afar. Invitations had gone out months in advance, and now Paris buzzed with anticipation. By early evening, the pâtisserie was transformed into a celebration of light, sound, and flavor. Garlands of sugar flowers adorned the entrances, and inside, an opulent display of pastries and pièces montées paid homage to Antoine's original art. Each station featured a creation that blended his classic techniques with modern influences, a testament to his belief that tradition and innovation could coexist beautifully.

At the center of it all stood Émile's *pièce montée*: a towering structure of golden caramel and delicate pastry, a sweeping, upward spiral inspired by the motion of a whisk, a symbol of transformation, of raw ingredients becoming something greater. Each tier told a story: the base, a foundation of classic techniques; the middle, an intricate lattice of pâte à choux and nougatine; and at the pinnacle, delicate petals of crystallized fruit, capturing both fragility and resilience. "It's breathtaking," whispered Clara, her earlier nerves replaced by awe. Émile adjusted a final detail, ensuring the balance was just right. "It represents movement, how we build on the past and push forward. Just as Antoine did."

As the evening unfolded, chefs and apprentices mingled their voices, a melody of admiration and excitement. Among the guests was Chef Haruto from Kyoto, known for his ethereal cherry blossom sugar domes. He stood beside Émile, lifting a glass in quiet reverence. "You have created something extraordinary," Haruto said. "Antoine's spirit is not only in this room but in all of us who continue to create." Nearby, Clara spoke with a visiting pastry chef from Buenos Aires. "Chef Émile believes in me," she said earnestly. "That's why I'm here, to be part of something bigger than myself." Chef Clara smiled. "That's what legacy does; it doesn't just preserve. It inspires us to build our own."

Long after the guests had departed and the kitchen had fallen silent, Émile stood alone in the main hall. The pièce montée shimmered under the soft glow of the chandeliers, a symbol of everything La Maison de Sucre had become. He carried Antoine's journal with him and stepped out onto the balcony for some air. The city stretched before him, its lights twinkling like stars. For a long moment, he stood still, the cool night air wrapping around him like a comforting embrace. Opening the journal, he turned to the last page, where Antoine's words waited:

"To create is to connect. To connect is to endure."

Émile closed the journal, lifting his head to the horizon. "We're still building your bridges, Chef," he murmured. "And we always will."

Voiceover (Émile): *"Creation is not an ending. It is a beginning, a flame that passes from hand to hand. Antoine taught us that beauty transcends time and that through our work, we are never truly gone."*

In the kitchen, Clara works quietly on her own design, her hands steady and sure proof that the spirit of what he left has been passed once again. The eternal table Antoine set continues to grow, its edges reaching farther than he ever could have imagined. And beneath it all flows the steady, unyielding current of inspiration, carrying forward the dreams of future generations.

CHAPTER 31
THE LEGACY MULTIPLIES

The spring air in Lyon carried a warmth that mirrored the city's energy—lively, bustling, and endlessly creative. The new La Maison de Sucre pâtisserie prepared for its grand opening. For Émile, this day marked both an achievement and a profound turning point. It was a step forward not just for the legacy of Antoine Carême but for the future he and his team hoped to shape. The decision to expand beyond Paris had been an emotional one, born from Émile's deep desire to continue sharing Antoine's dream with a broader audience while staying true to the traditions they guarded. Now, Lyon, a city steeped in culinary heritage, had welcomed them with open arms.

The Lyon location was a marvel of design, blending the elegance of La Maison de Sucre's Parisian charm with a modern sensibility. Walls of glass framed views of the city's twin rivers, the Rhône and Saône, their winding currents reflect time's passage and the blending of old and new. In the expansive kitchen, Émile moved among his team, the rhythm of their work grounding him as it always had. At the center of the room was Amelie, a fairly recent addition but extremely talented, now the head pâtissier of the Lyon location. Her leadership had been earned through years of dedication, patience, and unshakable drive. Where once she had been a nervous apprentice, she now commanded the kitchen with quiet confidence. "Everything ready, Amélie?" Émile asked, pausing beside her as she piped a final swirl of sugar glaze. She smiled, her hands steady. "Yes,

Chef. The pièce montée is nearly finished. I think Antoine would approve."

The centerpiece for the opening celebration was a sugar cathedral—an homage to Lyon's historic Basilica of Notre-Dame de Fourvière. Its towers gleamed with spun sugar, while the delicate sugar "stained glass" windows glowed with vibrant hues. Beneath it, a river of caramel flowed in tribute to the city's iconic waterways, symbolizing the merging of past and future. Émile's contemplation on the creation lingered with a look of lasting pride. "It's beautiful, Amélie. The spirit of this place and Antoine's vision shines through." "Thank you, Chef," she replied softly. "But we're building something new here, too. His legacy isn't just history—it's fuel for what comes next."

The Grand Opening

As evening descended, the Lyon pâtisserie came alive. Lanterns lit up the entrance, casting a warm, golden glow that spilled onto the cobbled streets. Inside, the air buzzed with excitement. Chefs, critics, and families gathered, eager to witness what La Maison de Sucre would bring to Lyon.

Amélie stood beside Émile, watching as guests marveled at the pastries and delicate confections lining the counters, each one a testament to what Antoine Carême had ignited. The pièce montée was unveiled to gasps of wonder, its intricate details drawing guests forward as if it held secrets waiting to be discovered. A young pastry chef from Lyon approached Amélie in awe. "How did you learn to do this?" she asked, her voice trembling with admiration. Amélie smiled, recognizing in the girl's expression the same spark she had once felt. "By watching, failing, and believing in the work's beauty. You can learn, too, if you're willing to try." The girl's face lit up. "One day, I'll make something as beautiful as this." Amélie placed a reassuring hand on the girl's shoulder. "You will. This is only the beginning."

As the celebrations died down and the last guests departed, Émile stepped outside to find Amélie standing at the edge of the terrace, overlooking the Rhône. The river glowed under the moonlight, its steady flow a comforting constant. "It's been a good day," Amélie said, her voice soft but full of emotion. Émile, while fixated on the water. "Yes. A new chapter. Amélie turned to look at him, searching his face. "Do you ever think about what he would say if he saw all of this?" Émile's forming a faint smile. "I think he'd remind us that the work isn't finished. That creation is a journey, not a destination." He reached into his coat pocket and pulled out a small, worn notebook, one of Antoine's original journals. Flipping to a page he had marked, he handed it to Amélie.

"To teach is to build bridges, connecting our past to the infinite possibilities of the future."

Amélie read the words, her breath catching. "That's exactly what we're doing, isn't it?" Émile nodded. "It's what Antoine did, what Juliette did, and now what we do. We build bonds, one pastry, creation, and dream at a time."

Voiceover (Émile):

"Antoine Carême understood that his work was not for himself but for those who would come after him. He knew that legacy is not a monument built in stone but a bridge that connects generations. It is alive, passed from hand to hand, carried forward with every act of creation."

Back in Paris, the original La Maison de Sucre, its kitchens were as vibrant as ever. Plans were underway to expand further, not replicate, but adapt Antoine's vision to new cultures and traditions. In Japan, a collaboration with a Kyoto pâtisserie explored the delicate harmony between French and Japanese confections. In Spain, chefs experimented with sugar work that paid homage to both Antoine's style and Spanish craftsmanship. In New York, a new location was being prepared, modern, bold, and rooted in the same spirit that Antoine had embodied so long ago. Émile sat alone at his desk in the Paris pâtisserie, surrounded by books, sketches, and journals that spanned centuries. He thought of Antoine, the boy who had sketched sugar palaces by candlelight, the man who had served kings, and the teacher who fills the hearts of countless chefs. Opening a blank journal, Émile began to write:

"Our work is not ours to keep. It belongs to those who dream beyond our reach, who see what we cannot yet imagine. In them, we endure. In them, we live forever."

Émile, standing, walked out and onto a bridge overlooking the Seine, the journal in hand. Across the water, La Maison de Sucre glows warmly, its lights reflecting on the river's surface. In Lyon, Amélie stood on the terrace of the new pâtisserie, her gaze observing the Rhône, a quiet smile on her lips. The final words resonate like a promise:

"The table Antoine set will always have room for more hands, voices, and visionaries. What came before will continue to shape the future, passed down through those who create and inspire."

CHAPTER 32
TWO HUNDRED YEARS OF SWEETNESS

Paris was alive with a sense of celebration that felt as if the city it-self understood the magnitude of the moment. Streets were decorated with colorful banners, musicians played at every corner, and the air was filled with the unmistakable aroma of pastries and caramelized sugar. Across the globe, in cities from Tokyo to New York, events were being held in tribute to Antoine Carême. The occasion marked 200 Years of Sweetness—the bicentennial of Antoine's birth and a celebration of the fire he had ignited two centuries ago.

At the nucleus of it all stood La Maison de Sucre, both in Paris and Lyon. The pâtisseries had become more than landmarks; they were beacons of love, connection, and legacy. Within their walls, the kitchens buzzed with life, Antoine's spirit enduring as an unbroken flame, inspiring each generation.

In Paris, Émile led his team with quiet determination, each movement in the kitchen deliberate as they prepared for the unveiling of their *pièce montée*. In Lyon, Amélie and her young apprentices mirrored the same sense of purpose, their hands steady, their focus unwavering. Though separated by distance, they worked toward a single vision, a tribute that would bring Antoine's influence full circle, celebrating not just his past but the future he had inspired.

The Parisian centerpiece was a breathtaking recreation of the Roman Colosseum, a tribute to Antoine's fascination with grandeur and structure. Its towering arches and curved walls were sculpted from golden nougatine, each detail meticulously rendered to reflect the strength and beauty of the ancient structures. Delicate columns of caramelized sugar gleamed in the light, their translucent amber hues evoking the sunlit stone of the original monument. At its base, intricate sugar figures stood frozen in time: chefs in crisp coats, artisans wielding whisks and rolling pins, and dreamers with hands outstretched as if reaching for the impossible. Each figure was a tribute to those who had carried the flame of culinary artistry from Antoine's era to the present. Around the structure, delicate sugar petals cascaded in soft spirals, a poetic reminder that time moves forward yet never erases the past.

As the final piece was set into place, Émile stepped back, studying the creation before him. It was more than a tribute. It was a statement, an acknowledgment that artistry, innovation, and passion were not bound to one man or one moment. They lived on, carried by the hands of those willing to build upon them, shaping the world one creation at a time.

In Lyon, Amélie's pièce montée took the form of a cathedral of light, its sugar-stained glass windows glowing from within. Delicate arches stretched skyward while rivers of caramel and marzipan wove through its foundation, a homage to both Lyon's rivers and the enduring flow of Antoine's dream.

As evening fell, La Maison de Sucre in Paris welcomed a global gathering of chefs, historians, and admirers. Faces from across cultures and continents filled the space, their voices a harmonious blend of languages and laughter. The energy was palpable, a shared understanding that they were part of something greater than themselves. Émile stood at the entrance, his emotions full of immense happiness as he greeted old friends and new faces. Among them were rising pastry chefs, culinary scholars, and the descendants of Antoine's first apprentices. For Émile, it was a moment of both pride and humility. "Chef Émile!" A voice broke through the crowd. A young woman approached, holding a well-worn copy of L'Art de la Cuisine Française. "I came from Montreal to be here today. My grandmother gave me this book when I was a child. She said it taught her that food could be art. And now, I'm here because of you and Antoine." Émile smiled warmly, his voice carrying the weight of the moment. "Antoine Carême believed that every creation carries a part of its maker. That book, his work, is alive in you now. Carry it forward."

As the hour arrived, the crowd gathered around the pièce montée, their whispers falling to silence as the curtains were drawn back. A sense of wonder filled the room. The Roman Colosseum sparkled in the glow of chandeliers, its towering arches and curved walls of nougatine seeming almost alive. It was a vision of symmetry and grandeur, but more importantly, it was a story, a tribute to Antoine's beginnings and the enduring reach of his fire.

In Lyon, Amélie's cathedral was met with the same stunned awe. Guests marveled at the play of light through the sugar-stained glass, the vibrant colors casting reflections across the room like echoes of Antoine's creativity. For Amélie and her team, the unveiling was a quiet triumph, a symbol of what they had become under his guiding legacy.

Voiceover (Émile):

"Antoine Carême dreamed of more than sugar palaces and banquet halls. He dreamed of connection—of leaving behind a torch that others would carry. Tonight, we are the proof that dreams, when shared, become eternal."

The celebrations continued late into the evening, with both locations connected through a live broadcast. Screens at La Maison de Sucre in Paris showed the cathedral in Lyon, while Lyon's guests watched as the temple was unveiled in Paris. Across continents and time zones, kitchens and schools hosted their own celebrations, streaming in to be part of the global moment. Chefs from Tokyo, Buenos Aires, London, and New York presented their own tributes, dishes inspired by Antoine's philosophies but rooted in their local traditions. Each one was a testament to his influence, proof of the greatness he left. As the celebrations subsided, Émile reflected. In his hand one more time was Antoine's original notebook, its pages fragile with age, his face reflecting the quiet joy of the evening. "It's incredible, isn't it?" he said to himself. "How far his dream has come. Antoine taught us that creation isn't just about what we make; it's about what we share. Every generation has added to his memory, carrying it into places he could never have imagined." He flipped to a page where Antoine's words stood bold and clear:

"To create is to endure. To endure is to connect. As long as beauty exists, so will those who seek to mold it."

Émile had taken a train to see Amélie the next day to see how she was and, at the same time, handed the notebook to Amélie. "It's your turn now," he said, his smile full of trust. "This gift is yours to carry forward." Amélie's hands trembled as she accepted the journal, with tears shimmering. "I'll protect it. And I'll make something new from it, just as he would have wanted."

As dawn broke over Paris and Lyon, light spilled across the windows of La Maison de Sucre, its glow a promise that the story was far from over. Inside both kitchens, young chefs had already begun their work, their hands moving with skill and purpose. Every whisk turned, every sugar spun, carried with it the spirit of Antoine Carême.

Voiceover (Émile):

"Legacy is not bound by time. It grows, changes, and multiplies with each generation. Antoine Carême's light is in every creation, every dream, every hand that shapes beauty from chaos."

The Seine in Paris and the Rhône in Lyon. The rivers flow steadily, carrying with them the dreams of generations past and present. Above them, La Maison de Sucre stands as a beacon of light, its kitchens alive with life and creation.

"Antoine Carême's light sparked a thousand others, spreading across kitchens, continents, and hearts. In every creation we shape, we add our voices to his eternal story."

EPILOGUE

Years turned to decades, and Antoine Carême's legacy grew even brighter. His name, etched into the history of gastronomy, became a beacon of innovation and refinement. Known as the "King of Chefs and the Chef of Kings," Carême's contributions to haute cuisine defined an era and influenced future generations. Carême's legacy began with his pioneering work in systematizing French cuisine. His meticulously detailed books, such as *L'Art de la Cuisine Française*, codified recipes, techniques, and even kitchen organization. These texts became the cornerstone of modern culinary education, studied by chefs worldwide. His skillfulness in creating towering pièces montées—architectural marvels of sugar and confection—transformed desserts into an art form, elevating the role of the pâtissier.

In Tokyo, a group of pastry chefs unveiled a sugar sculpture inspired by Carême's architectural designs. Their pièce montée, a delicate pagoda surrounded by cherry blossoms constructed from spun sugar, paid homage to Carême's ability to blend cultural influences into his art. The chefs remarked on how his philosophy of harmony between tradition and innovation resonated deeply with all of them.

In Buenos Aires, a chocolatier introduced a confection series called "Antoine's Dream," blending French techniques with Argentine flavors. The collection featured intricate sugarwork and drew from Carême's belief that desserts could tell a story, transcending borders and connecting people through taste.

In New York City, a new culinary institute named its main hall after Antoine Carême. This hall showcased a permanent exhibit of his life and work, including replicas of his most famous pièces montées and excerpts from his journals. Visitors marveled at the depth of his vision, finding inspiration in the pages where he once sketched sugar cathedrals and Grecian temples.

In Paris, La Maison de Sucre remained a shining beacon. Émile's successors had transformed it into a hub of creativity and education. Its dual roles as pâtisserie and institute inspired chefs from all around to innovate while respecting the traditions Antoine had codified. The kitchen walls bore reminders of his ethos: "Perfection is not a destination; it is a practice." On a quiet afternoon, one of Émile's apprentices, now a master chef herself, stood before a group of students. Her voice carried the weight of history as she spoke: "Antoine Carême taught us that food is more than sustenance. It is an expression of identity, a bridge between cultures, and a celebration of beauty. Every creation we make carries his spirit forward." The students, with their hands steady as they worked on sugar sculptures, their minds filled with the stories of the chef who had dared to dream.

Voiceover (Historian): "*Two centuries after his passing, Antoine Carême's vision is held in many who have followed in his footsteps. He redefined the role of the chef, transforming it into that of an artist and diplomat. His towering sugar sculptures, codification of French cuisine, and belief in the transformative power of beauty have transcended his time. Carême reminds us that the simplest act of creation can resonate across generations.*"

La Maison de Sucre on a crisp winter evening. Its windows glow warmly, and inside, chefs and apprentices work side by side, their laughter and focus filling the space with life. On a central wall hangs Antoine's original journal, its pages preserved as a testament to the spark that started it all.

Outside, the Seine flows steadily, its currents a reflection of time's unyielding march. Above, the stars twinkle like sugar crystals scattered across the night sky, a reminder that even the most fleeting creations can leave an enduring mark.

Final Voiceover: *"Antoine Carême's flame is not just his anymore. It burns in every hand that creates, every heart that dreams, and every table that gathers people together. His story is not an end, but a beginning—an eternal flame lighting the way for generations to come."*

ABOUT THE AUTHOR

Dorian Cainewell, a professional chef with nearly 20 years of experience in the culinary arts, hails from the vibrant city of Calgary, Alberta, Canada, where his family's roots run deep. For over a century, the Blackstone/Shumiatcher/Smith family has been an integral part of Calgary's history, shaping its cultural, legal, and artistic landscapes.

In the early 1900s, Dorian's great-great-grandfather arrived in Calgary, carrying with him the first Torah to the city—an enduring symbol of faith and tradition. His great-grandfather, Morris Shumiatcher-smith, further etched the family's name into Calgary's legacy by founding Smithbilt Hats, the company that created Calgary's most iconic symbol: the white cowboy hat, a beacon of the city's spirit and hospitality.

The family's influence continued through generations. From the 1960s to the 1990s, the Shumiatcher/Blackstone family left an indelible mark on Calgary's music scene, fostering a legacy of piano performance, appreciation, and education with Claira Blackstone, Dorian's grandfather, Irwin A. Blackstone, carried the family's inspirational torch into the legal world, becoming a respected member of the Alberta Law Society and serving as a provincial court judge. His contributions live on today through the Blackstone Debates, held annually at the University of Calgary—an event honoring his legacy of critical thinking and advocacy.

Inspired by this lineage of pioneers, visionaries, and creators, Dorian Cainewell seeks to carry forward his family's tradition of greatness by leaving his own mark—one that bridges the worlds of culinary art, storytelling, and history.

The Chef of Kings, The King of Chefs, Dorian's literary debut, celebrates the life and legacy of Antoine Marie Carême, a man heralded as the first *celebrity chef.* Through historical research and evocative storytelling, Dorian breathes life into Carême's journey—an artist whose culinary mastery not only elevated French cuisine but also laid the foundations for modern gastronomy. Dorian's work reflects his belief that history is more than facts and dates; it is a living, breathing force that connects generations and inspires greatness.

A storyteller at heart and a chef by trade, Dorian's dedication to his craft mirrors the spirit of his ancestors: to honor tradition while embracing innovation and create beauty that resonates beyond its time. He writes for audiences of all generations—from history and culinary buffs to lovers of timeless stories, inviting readers to savor the richness of lives once lived and the legacies they left behind.

On a personal note, Dorian's work pays tribute to his family's enduring spirit. Just as they shaped Calgary's identity, Dorian seeks to shape his own legacy—one of art, perseverance, and inspiration.

HISTORICAL REFERENCES

1. Antoine Carême's Writings

- Carême, Antoine. *L'Art de la Cuisine Française au Dix-Neuvième Siècle*. A cornerstone in shaping the culinary philosophy and techniques depicted in this novel.

- Primary insights into Carême's innovative approach to haute cuisine and his role as an early advocate for the artistic potential of cooking.

2. Biographical Studies

- Kelly, Ian. *Cooking for Kings: The Life of Antonin Carême, the First Celebrity Chef*. A comprehensive exploration of Carême's life, with details about his professional accomplishments and the political landscape he navigated.

- Wheaton, Barbara Ketcham. *Savoring the Past: The French Kitchen and Table from 1300 to 1789*. Contextual background on the evolution of French cuisine, aiding in the depiction of Carême's revolutionary impact.

3. Historical Context

- Price, Roger. *A Concise History of France*. Used to contextualize the Napoleonic era, the Bourbon Restoration, and the socio-political dynamics influencing Carême's patrons.

- Gooch, Brison. *The Congress of Vienna, 1814-1815*. Provided insight into the cultural and diplomatic significance of Carême's role in European politics.

Culinary Research

1. Haute Cuisine and French Culinary Traditions

- Escoffier, Auguste. *Le Guide Culinaire.* While written after Carême's time, this work provided a framework for understanding the lasting influence of his techniques.

- Root, Waverley and de Rochemont, Samuel. *The Food of France.* A culinary historian's view on the regional flavors and techniques that shaped French cuisine.

2. Sugar Art and Pastry Techniques

- Modern works on sugar sculpting and pastry provided insight into the technical challenges Carême might have faced in creating his famed pièces montées.

- Visual resources from museums and culinary archives for detailed descriptions of period-specific confectionery tools and techniques.

Creative and Interpretative Tools

1. Fictional Elements

- While based on Carême's documented life and achievements, creative liberties were taken to imagine personal relationships, dialogues, and inner thoughts that align with historical context but remain speculative.

- Research into character archetypes from historical fiction for crafting multidimensional secondary characters.

2. Architecture and Design

- Studies of period architecture, including Paris landmarks like Notre-Dame and the Palais-Royal, informed the detailed descriptions of Carême's pièces montées.

- Online archives of architectural sketches from the 18th and 19th centuries for inspiration in depicting sugar sculptures.

Acknowledgments to Resources

1. Artistic Inspiration

- Discussions with contemporary pastry chefs that helped bridge the historical narrative with modern culinary innovation.

2. General Historical Context

- Encyclopedia Britannica entries on Napoleon Bonaparte, Tsar Alexander I, and King George IV provided a broader understanding of Carême's patrons and their political worlds.

www.ingramcontent.com/pod-product-compliance
Lightning Source LLC
Chambersburg PA
CBHW041828090426
42811CB00038B/2360/J